COMING HOME

COMING HOME

How Black Americans Will Re-Elect Trump

VERNON ROBINSON III
BRUCE EBERLE

Humanix Books
www.humanixbooks.com

Humanix Books

COMING HOME

Humanix Books, P.O. Box 20989, West Palm Beach, FL 33416, USA
www.humanixbooks.com | info@humanixbooks.com

ISBN: 978-163006-141-8 (Hardcover)
ISBN: 978-163006-143-2 (E-book)

Printed in the United States of America

10 9 8 7 6 5 4 3 2 1

For Dr. Stella Pecot Robinson, who risked her life registering voters in the South in the 1940s and who never let fear or intimidation deter her from fighting for the freedom of her children yet unborn, and for Vernon Robinson, Jr., a valiant Tuskegee Airman who defeated fascism abroad and paved the way to desegregate the armed forces at home. They are among the thousands of unsung heroes who worked hard to secure full rights for African Americans. Thank you, Mom and Dad, for instilling in me a love of country and passing the torch of freedom along to me.

—Vernon Robinson III

And, for Connor, Andrew, Sean and Ryan Livingstone. May you enjoy and appreciate the freedom that millions before you have worked and sacrificed so much to preserve. God willing, your generation will be up to the task of defending and preserving freedom for those who come after you. May those efforts be blessed with success.

—Bruce Eberle

Contents

INTRODUCTION

At just 28 years of age, Abraham Lincoln understood where the real danger to our republic would come from. He presciently spoke these words before the Young Men's Lyceum of Springfield, Illinois, on January 27, 1838:

> At what point shall we expect the approach of danger? By what means shall we fortify against it? Shall we expect some transatlantic military giant, to step the Ocean, and crush us at a blow? Never! All the armies of Europe, Asia and Africa combined, with all the treasure of the earth (our own excepted) in their military chest; with a Buonaparte for a commander, could not by force, take a drink from the Ohio, or make a track on the Blue Ridge, in a trial of a thousand years. At what point then is the approach of danger to be expected? I answer, if it ever reach us, it must spring up amongst us. It cannot come from abroad. If destruction be our lot, we must ourselves be its author and finisher.[1]

In this address, Lincoln was of course referring to the danger of America being torn apart by a civil war, which in fact took place just 23 years later. Indeed, on November 19, 1863, after the bloody battle at Gettysburg, Lincoln began his address to the gathered crowd with these words that defined the essence of the struggle:

> Four score and seven years ago our fathers brought forth on this continent, a new nation, conceived in Liberty, and

> dedicated to the proposition that all men are created equal. Now we are engaged in a great civil war, testing whether that nation, or any nation so conceived and so dedicated, can long endure.[2]

Although there are no men or women dying in violent battles on American soil today, the danger to the existence of our republic posed by those on the extreme left has never been greater. There can be no doubt that we are engaged in a battle for the soul of America and for the virtues and values that make freedom possible. The question that Lincoln posed in the Gettysburg Address remains: Can "any nation so conceived and so dedicated" long endure?

The sad truth is that the once great Democratic Party, the party of Franklin Roosevelt, Harry Truman, John F. Kennedy, and yes, Bill Clinton, has been hijacked by radical leftists who despise our Founders, reject our republican form of government, spurn traditional American values, and seek to impose cradle-to-grave government control over our lives. Formerly relegated to the fringe of American politics, these far-left radicals have seized control of today's Democratic Party. Old line liberal Democrats such as Nancy Pelosi have made a deal with the Devil by allowing these dangerous radicals into their party, and we are witnessing the disaster that will befall America if these radicals complete their takeover of the U.S. government.

These new radical Democrats espouse a particularly harsh form of socialism and all-powerful government that is sure to lead to the end of America as we know it. Because they are unable to understand that imperfect human beings will never create a perfect society, they reject the idea that America was ever great.[3] They seek not a better society but a perfect society, a utopia. No one would ever argue that America has not had deep, ugly flaws, slavery and segregation being by far the most notable. But thanks to great leaders such as Abraham Lincoln and Dr. Martin Luther King, Jr., Americans bled and died to bring such hideous tragedies to an end. Of course, America still has its imperfections and always will, because America, like every other nation, is populated by imperfect people, people with human flaws. This understanding of human nature was part of the genius of the Founders.[4] They endeavored to create a government with checks and balances that would limit the power of any individual or any political party, knowing that too much power in the hands of any person would be a threat to individual freedom.

But these radicals who either don't believe in God or see no use for Him reject the idea that human nature cannot be improved. Like all would-be dictators before them—Robespierre, Lenin, Stalin, Hitler, Mussolini, Pol Pot, Mao, Castro, Chávez, Maduro, Ortega—they believe that they can create the perfect society. The dreams of such utopians always lead to the nightmare of dictatorship that ends the rule of law, chokes off human freedom, and creates universal misery and poverty. As Ben Shapiro put it, *"Those systems of thought, in the absence of God, end with the gulags, they end with the gas chambers. They end in terrible places."*[5]

Repelling this threat to the United States and to our republican form of government is the challenge of our times. It is a battle that must be joined by every freedom-loving American if our children and grandchildren are to enjoy the liberty, civility, decency, and prosperity we inherited from those who came before us.

To be clear, this book is not just about resisting the onslaught of these dangerous radicals but about triumphing over them. We believe that a big step toward that goal can happen in 2020 if Donald Trump wins in a historic landslide that repudiates socialism and decimates today's radical Democratic Party. Working together, we believe we can overwhelmingly defeat these radicals and drive them back into the fringes of America's political landscape, where they belong.

Why are the authors of this book so certain that Donald Trump can rout the radical left in 2020? The answer is a secret that we learned from studying the 2016 presidential campaign. It is the key to a sweeping win by Donald Trump in 2020. On the surface it sounds almost innocuous, but the political ramifications are nothing less than earthshaking. This is what we learned.

In 2016, for the first time in nearly 60 years, a Republican candidate for president, Donald J. Trump, received more than 20 percent of the black vote in the key swing state of Pennsylvania. More than 140,000 black Pennsylvanians voted for Trump, making it possible for him to be elected president of the United States.[6] That's right: Black Americans not only gave Donald Trump his margin of victory in Pennsylvania but did the same thing in the key state of Michigan. In reality, it was black Americans who made the election of President Trump possible.

Skeptics may cite the fact that in 2016 a number of all-black precincts in Philadelphia voted 100 percent for Hillary Clinton. That is true. However, those on welfare and in poverty in those precincts account for just 21.2 percent of the total black population.[7] The remaining 78.8 percent of the black population, those who have jobs, live as far away as possible from those dangerous areas. Black Americans who are working and are above the poverty line were clearly the source of Trump's support in 2016.

Why is this so politically earthshaking? Donald Trump winning 20 percent or more of the black vote makes the election of any Democratic candidate for president nearly impossible. But how reliable is the survey that indicates that Trump won more than 20 percent of the black vote in Pennsylvania? So far as we are aware, the results of the poll we are referring to have never before been released to the public, but it was taken just four days before the 2016 election. It had a margin of error of ±1.89 percent with a 95 percent level of confidence. This means that the sample of black voters was large enough to make the survey statistically valid within the range indicated and that it contained a proportional representation of voters at all income levels.

There is no doubt that a dramatic turnaround by black voters provides the key to victory by Donald Trump in 2020. In the pages that follow, we explain why Donald Trump exceeded 20 percent support from black Americans in Pennsylvania and also received record black support for a Republican candidate for president in other swing states. The last Republican candidate for president to receive more than 20 percent of the black vote in a presidential election was Richard Nixon in 1960.[8] More to the point, if Donald Trump wins 20 percent of the black vote in 2020, he is virtually guaranteed a landslide victory. Such a victory will set back radical leftists for decades. It will result in internal fighting inside the Democratic Party like we have never seen before and may split that party in half, destroying its plan to establish a permanent Democratic majority.[9]

But why did Donald Trump receive more than 20 percent of the black vote in Pennsylvania, and why is black support for the president likely to grow well beyond that level in other states in 2020? Does this signal a historic remigration of black support from the Democratic Party back to the Republican Party? Are there signs of such a shift? What are the similarities between black support for Donald Trump and black support for Franklin D. Roosevelt? Although they were dramatically different in their approach to government, what is it that Roosevelt and Trump have in common? Today there are hundreds of black conservative leaders across America holding elective office, leading organizations, writing for major publications, and appearing on television and radio. What caused this to happen? Will 2020 be a watershed year for Donald Trump and the black vote, as it was for FDR in 1936? If that is to happen, what must take place to make it happen?

There are other important questions that we will answer, such as, why didn't the conservative movement encourage and support the civil rights movement of the 1950s and 1960s? What price have conservatives paid for that lack of support? Who made the integration of baseball, America's leading spectator sport at that time, possible? Which courageous U.S. senator opened the Senate cafeteria to black Americans? What is the little-known story behind

Senator Barry Goldwater's decision to vote against the Civil Rights Act of 1964? Similarly, why have liberals recently reverted to their original progressive moniker in honor of President Woodrow Wilson? Why have Democrats dropped Andrew Jackson as the father of the modern Democratic Party? These are just a few of the questions that will be answered in this book, but make no mistake, the central focus of the book is to illuminate a path to a big win for Donald Trump in 2020.

Our goal is not to rehash the past failings of those in positions of power who made promise after promise to black America only to act counter to those promises. Yes, we briefly recount them, but if we simply pointed out these failings and went no further, this book would not have served its intended purpose.

Make no mistake, it is extremely unlikely that a *majority* of black Americans will vote for Donald Trump in 2020. But it is an undeniable fact that black voters are restless and dissatisfied with the lack of progress they have made under Democratic leadership over the last 80 years. As data and events indicate, black voters are definitely taking a second look at Donald Trump. In fact, as we will show, a sizable number of black Americans have already left the Democratic Party plantation.

Nevertheless, this book is about the future; however, to get to the future, we need to begin with an appraisal of how we got where we are today. Then there has to be to a road map explaining how to persuade 20 percent or more of black Americans to vote for Donald Trump in 2020.

One thing is obvious: When a political party must consistently win 90 percent or even 95 percent of the black vote to succeed, that party is in a precarious political situation. That's the politically dangerous position the Democratic Party finds itself in today. That's why ridiculous charges that Donald Trump is a racist or even a white supremacist are so over the top and so easily refuted. But just rejecting such attacks is not enough, as we shall explain. Today's vicious attacks claiming that Donald Trump and all conservatives are racist are so shrill, outrageous, and unhinged not because the attackers believe they are true but because they know they are untrue. In breathless, hyperventilating anger they spew forth such smears because they fear they are losing the black vote. They should be worried, because they are.

If you are a Democrat, how do you maintain almost complete allegiance from black voters for more than 80 years? You can't rely on issues because your agenda runs counter to the beliefs of nearly half of all black voters. So what do you do? You manufacture a narrative that all Republicans, especially Donald Trump, are racists. You tell lies. You create myths. You yell it from the housetops. You run radio, TV, and social media ads screaming that all Republicans are racist. In short, you terrorize black Americans, telling them that if you elect a Republican, America will return to segregation or worse. But the problem with crying wolf all the time is that it loses credibility, especially when the policies of Trump have benefited black Americans more than the policies of any other president in recent history. Trump and his policies have clearly broken through with black voters. That's a big problem for the Democrats and their allies in the news media.

As a final note, the reader should know that the authors struggled with two terms in writing this book. The first is what name to use for Americans of African descent. The problem is that within the time span this book covers, these Americans have been identified by various writers, authors, and historians with different terms during different periods of American history. Similarly, those Americans of African descent also have used different words to identify members of their race at various points in time. These descriptive words include *colored*, *Negro*, *Afro American*, and today, *African American* or *black American*. The U.S. Census Bureau uses the term *black American* in its publications, and that's the reason the authors have chosen to use that term throughout the book. We are not arguing that it is the best term or the most logical term or the most preferred term. It is simply a descriptive term, although admittedly it is a human construction. We recognize that the Bible makes no reference to multiple races; it only refers to the human race, and that is one term we can all agree on. We are all brothers and sisters who are equal in the sight of God.

Our only exception to using the term *black American* is when direct quotes are used. In such cases we understandably use whatever the original author chose, even if it is vile and ugly (in such cases we clearly identify what the word was, but we don't actually use it). The one thing we seek is honesty, and history shows that some of the facts are brutal.

The second predicament we faced was deciding whether to use the word *progressive* or the word *liberal* to describe those on the left side of the American political spectrum. *Progressive* was the descriptive term that was first used in America in the 1890s to describe those on the left, but by World War II that term had been discarded in favor *liberal.* Apparently, this was done because the term *progressive* was associated with ideas, programs, and plans that were increasingly unpopular. However, today the descriptive term of *liberal* has also become politically unpopular, and so recently liberals decided that they would once again prefer the term *progressive.* This presented the authors with a dilemma: Which descriptive term—*liberal* or *progressive*—is most appropriate and practical to identify those on the left over the time span covered in this book? The choice is made even more difficult by the fact that the transition in terms from *liberal* to *progressive* seems to still be in progress. In light of the fact that the transition is still under way, the authors chose to alternately or in combination use both terms as seems appropriate in a particular instance. Again, in direct quotes, the term used by the authors of those quotes is used.

Finally, we did our best not to overstate the events no matter how outrageous they might have been at the time. If we were not convinced of the veracity of the stories told or the words spoken, we did not include them. Although both authors are conservatives who have taken strong positions on political and cultural issues, our goal is a truthful story of the history of black Americans and their relationship to Republicans, Democrats, conservatives, and liberals, letting the chips fall where they may. The bottom line is that we wrote this book through the lens of the 2020 presidential election. We're confident that there is no other book that documents and explains why Donald Trump has a landslide victory within his reach in 2020.

CHAPTER 1

Donald Trump's Party

When Donald Trump came down the escalator at Trump Tower on June 16, 2015, and announced that he was a candidate for president of the United States, the authors of this book were not only skeptical but dismissive. We were both heavily involved in a super PAC supporting Ben Carson for president. Dr. Carson was running ahead of every other candidate, and we certainly did not see Donald Trump as a threat to him. We could not have been more wrong. Trump quickly shot to the top of the polls and stayed there until he won the Republican nomination for president at the Cleveland convention of the GOP.

Even after Trump was the Republican nominee for president we were not enthralled. We were both certain that he was not a conservative and that with his past record of being a Democrat, if elected, he would be at best a moderate Republican in the mold of Gerald Ford and George H. W. Bush—a president without a governing philosophy who would be on the left on one topic, be on the right on another topic, and mostly muddle in the middle. Nevertheless, we voted for Trump and worked for Trump because we knew he would be better than Hillary Clinton. We knew that if Hillary packed the Supreme Court with liberal jurists, the U.S. Constitution would quickly become meaningless and the rights of all Americans, especially God-fearing Americans, would be circumscribed. In short, we worked for and voted for Donald Trump because we saw him as the lesser of two evils.

We were wrong about Donald Trump again. Once elected, he not only picked members of the federal judiciary, including the Supreme Court, from a list put together by the Federalist Society, he also put Vice President Mike Pence in charge of his transition team, which was packed with folks from the Heritage Foundation. Also, his foreign policy turned out to be more in line with conservative icon Robert Taft than with the military adventurism of George W. Bush.

Unlike any other Republican president before him, Trump insisted that our allies in Europe start paying more of the cost of maintaining their defense through the North Atlantic Treaty Organization (NATO). As his administration took charge, he cut taxes, he slashed regulations,[10] he ended the Obamacare personal mandate[11] and put that albatross of a program on life support, and he has done more than any president since Eisenhower to secure our southern border.

Although some Never Trumpers on the right didn't support the president and still don't, the overwhelming majority of conservatives are now fully behind his economic, domestic, and foreign policies. In fact, today the number of conservatives who do not support Donald Trump is so small as to be politically insignificant. Their argument that Donald Trump is not a philosophical conservative may be true, but according to Tommy Binion, who is responsible for the advocacy of policies set forth by the Heritage Foundation, *"At the end of 2017, we reviewed all 334 recommendations presented in our 'Mandate for Leadership' series and found that the Trump administration had embraced fully 64 percent of them. That's nearly two out of three—and that's very good indeed."*[12] Exactly how good is Trump's performance according to the Heritage Foundation? Kay Coles James, Heritage's president, said in a speech[13] that in eight years Ronald Reagan was able to fulfill less than 50 percent of the goals set forth in the Mandate for Leadership book prepared for the Reagan administration. Of course, Reagan often faced a hostile Congress, whereas Donald Trump had a somewhat supportive Republican Congress during the first two years of his administration.

There's no doubt that today's Republican Party is Donald Trump's Republican Party, and to a greater or lesser extent he is the leader of today's conservative movement. To put it another way, *"there's no longer any doubt that the conservative movement has been redefined by President Trump, leaving him with a fiercely loyal base of support as he prepares for a 2020 re-election campaign."*[14] On many fronts, Donald Trump has followed historical conservative positions, reducing the power of government by eliminating more than 30,000 pages of regulations,[15] creating a booming economy by reducing taxes, dramatically rebuilding our military power, pursuing a foreign policy of peace through strength, exiting the dreadful Paris accords (the climate change agreement), getting America out of the ill-conceived Iran deal orchestrated by President Obama, and enabling the United States to achieve energy independence by encouraging energy production and the building of pipelines.

But on other fronts, Trump has undertaken policies heretofore not espoused by traditional conservatives and establishment Republicans, such as asserting strong pressure on NATO nations to pay their fair share for their own defense;[16] working hard to protect Americans by building a wall on our southern border; advocating for immigration reform based on merit; using tariffs to negotiate better trade deals with China, Mexico, and other nations; and advocating for infrastructure rebuilding. Slowly but surely, conservatives are moving toward these new policies, understanding that our European allies are not paying their fair share to defend themselves, that we need a secure southern border, and that America does require an influx of legal immigrants who bring something to our nation. However, too many members of the Republican establishment continue to resist Trump's commonsense policies. Globalist Republicans fight against border security because they rely on money from the Chamber of Commerce and its members who want the cheap labor that is available when our borders are open. This old guard Republican establishment is a member in good standing of the Washington, D.C., swamp that Donald Trump is trying to drain. Ironically, the truth is that when it comes to free trade, it is clear that Donald Trump is actually doing more to achieve free and fair trade by using tariffs to create a level trading field than traditional conservatives and establishment Republicans have ever done.

There is one more thing that has the Republican establishment up in arms, and that is the effort by Trump to end the military adventurism of previous presidents, including Republican presidents. Failed nation-building schemes have cost American taxpayers trillions of dollars and have not brought the world any closer to peace. Donald Trump is a realist and knows that the United States cannot be the policeman to the world or spread democracy across the globe. And although Republican politicians succumb to political correctness, Donald Trump has taken this abridgement of free speech head-on. Whereas previous Republican and Democrat presidents pledged to move the American embassy in Israel to Jerusalem, Trump actually did it to the chagrin of many, if not most, members of the Washington, D.C., swamp.

Inheriting a military quagmire in the Middle East, Trump ignored the big brass at the Pentagon and talked directly to the field generals and the sergeants fighting on the ground in Iraq.[17] As a result, the gloves were taken off our fighting men and women, making it possible for the United States to destroy ISIS in a matter of months instead of years. His years of experience building a multi-billion-dollar corporation have taught him to bypass those at the top and speak directly with the men and women on the ground who really know what is going on. No wonder he is known as the "blue-collar billionaire."[18]

Whereas other presidents have taken action only after years of deliberation and political calculation, Donald Trump has a bias for action. That has made it possible to rebuild our military by pumping an additional $160 billion[19] into the Pentagon budget. His economic policies have resulted in more than 6 million new jobs,[20] 491,000 of which are manufacturing jobs,[21] jobs that former president Barack Obama said *"aren't coming back."*[22] In fact, according to a *Barron's Market Watch* headline, *"Manufacturing jobs [are] growing at fastest rate in 23 years."*[23] That's *"more than six times the 73,000 manufacturing jobs added in Obama's last two years."*[24]

Whereas previous Republican presidents have virtually ignored the real needs of black Americans or parroted the failed policies of the Democrats, who offer a handout instead of a hand up, Donald Trump has become a champion of black Americans. He has brought black unemployment to the lowest point in recorded history,[25] and his policies have made it possible for black-owned businesses to increase by 400 percent in just one year.[26] In the Oval Office and across the nation, President Trump has gone on the ground to see what needs to be done to help black Americans in poverty climb America's amazing economic ladder of success. He is determined to restore the strong bond that Republicans had with black Americans before the time of Franklin D. Roosevelt.

Donald Trump believes that black economic success is crucial if America is to achieve racial harmony that benefits all races. And as a by-product of black economic success and the actions he has taken, Trump is convinced that black voters will rally to him in 2020. He is not satisfied with winning just a few votes from these fellow Americans; President Trump wants to win a majority of the black vote. That's unlikely to happen in 2020, but already, through Trump's direct, candid approach, black Americans are taking a serious second look at him and his policies. Even as the Democrats falsely accuse him of being a racist, Trump has begun the long overdue effort to reestablish trust with the black American community. As a result of his economic policies, nearly 6 million Americans have been able to get off food stamp dependency.[27]

To put it bluntly, most Republican presidents since but not including Richard Nixon have simply ignored the black community. It's not that their policies weren't helpful to the black community, it's just that they were told by inside-the-Beltway political consultants in Washington, D.C., that their best course of action was to stay quiet and ignore black Americans, especially in an election year. They were told that appealing to black voters would only increase the black turnout and thus aid the Democrats more than the Republicans.

But Donald Trump didn't come from Washington, D.C. He didn't want to become a Washington, D.C., insider; he wanted to change the way things are done inside the Beltway. In his entire business career, he has been a disrupter, someone who shakes things up and gets things done. He appealed to Democratic blue-collar workers because he wanted to bring manufacturing jobs back to America, and he has. He appealed to evangelical Christians because he promised to defend Christianity and Christians, and he has.[28] And because he appealed directly to black Americans, they supported him more strongly in key swing states than they supported any Republican candidate in the last 50 years.[29] Trump received strong support from small business owners because he understood their challenges and promised to address them. He did. Trump received strong military and veteran support because he promised to rebuild America's military and clear up the mess in VA hospitals. He did both. And because Trump promised to restore prosperity, he received stronger support from Hispanic Americans than did Mitt Romney four years earlier, receiving 29 percent of the Hispanic vote, and recent polls indicate that if the election were held now, he would receive 49 percent of the Hispanic vote.[30] He is especially popular with Hispanics who fled socialist dictatorships in Cuba, Nicaragua, and Venezuela.

Donald Trump may not be a philosophical conservative, but clearly he has wonderful conservative instincts along with a populist perspective that is not dissimilar to that of the late Jack Kemp. We are not, of course, suggesting that Trump has the same temperament as Kemp, but Trump's strong desire to be the president of every American regardless of race, religion, ethnic background, or any other trait has made him popular with all races and ethnic groups. He rejects the foolish idea that diversity is the strength of America and understands that assimilation and unity are the strength of America.

There's no doubt that Donald Trump has achieved great success as president in his first term, rebuilding the economy, taking concrete steps to lift the poor out of poverty, restoring respect for America around the globe, appointing judges dedicated to the Constitution, and standing up to attacks on Christianity. But who is Donald Trump the man? Yes, he is a serial exaggerator, as Brit Hume put it.[31] He is bold and strong and at times painfully candid, even abrasive. But what are his values? What does he believe in?

The best explanation of the values of Donald Trump is found in the book by David Brody and Scott Lamb, *The Faith of Donald J. Trump*.[32] Brody and Lamb extensively researched the Trump family, tracing its history back into Germany, the home of the Trumps, and back to the Isle of Lewis in Scotland, where Donald's mother came from. They also examine the faith of Donald Trump, his values, and his work ethic. One takeaway from their book is that Trump is a 1950s man, or as Victor Davis Hansen put it, *"Trump seemed a Rip Van Winkle. He was waking up from a 1950s slumber into an unrecognizable culture."*[33] What does it mean to be a 1950s man? Simply put, it means that Donald Trump is an old-fashioned patriot who loves America, loves all Americans, and reveres the Founders of America. He cares about people, and when it comes to race, he is as color-blind as a human can be. Donald Trump believes in and respects the police and the military. He may not be a conservative, but he is a proud American through and through. He works hard, and he treats people with respect. Those who work for him and work with him clearly like him. In business he greatly values talent and doesn't care if the person is male or female, black, white, Asian, or Hispanic. While running the Trump organization, he even received praise from Jesse Jackson for being a leader in race relations and opportunity for black Americans.[34] There are hardworking, talented men and women, black and white, throughout the Trump organization and at all levels of leadership. He also is strongly influenced by the evangelical Christians with whom he meets regularly in the White House.

Donald Trump comes to his views via patriotism and common sense. That's why he is today the de facto leader of the Republican Party and the conservative movement. That is good because he knows how to win and bad because whatever baggage the conservative movement carries is automatically associated with him. Therein lies a problem because those in the conservative movement do carry baggage when it comes to their history with black Americans, specifically their inaction during the days of the civil rights movement of the 1950s and 1960s.

CHAPTER 2

Conservative Failure

If Donald Trump wins 20 or even 30 percent of the black vote, he will have taken a major step toward reestablishing the nearly unbreakable alliance black Americans had with the Republican Party for more than 70 years after the assassination of Abraham Lincoln. However, to do so, he must end the division that has existed between Republicans and black Americans since 1964. To understand how he can do that, we must first understand how this parting of the ways occurred.

From the beginning, the Republican Party was antislavery; in fact, the election of its first president, Abraham Lincoln, precipitated a bloody Civil War for the purpose not only of preserving the Union but also of freeing the slaves. Of course, it was during that war that Lincoln issued the Emancipation Proclamation, which declared freedom for the slaves. On January 31, 1865, shortly before his assassination, Lincoln orchestrated passage of the Thirteenth Amendment to the U.S. Constitution, which ended slavery forever. From 1870 when the Fifteenth Amendment was passed, until 1936, black Americans voted overwhelmingly for Republican candidates for president. But in 1964, with the nomination of Barry Goldwater, who voted against the passage of the 1964 Civil Rights Act, black voters abandoned the Republican Party and its conservative candidates, seemingly forever.

Today, most Republicans and conservatives are frustrated by this abandonment. They can't understand why black voters reject their candidates. They wonder why their candidates typically receive just 5 to 10 percent of the black vote. In exasperation, they say something like "I don't understand it. We support the issues that a significant percent of black voters support. For decades the polls have shown that about one-third of black voters agree with us on all the issues. Why, then, don't one-third of black voters support us?"

There are two reasons black Americans don't vote for conservative candidates. The first reason is trust. The overwhelming majority of black Americans simply don't trust conservatives and Republicans, and their mistrust is understandable. It goes back to Richard Nixon's unwillingness to call the Atlanta judge who threatened to put Dr. Martin Luther King, Jr., in a notoriously dangerous prison after Nixon was asked to make the call by Martin Luther King, Sr. It goes back to Senator Barry Goldwater's vote against the 1964 Civil Rights Act. Most of all, it goes back to the absence of conservative support for the civil rights struggle of the late 1950s and 1960s.

At that time, William F. Buckley, Jr., was the undisputed leader of the conservative movement. He was an intellectual giant and a man of great wisdom. He not only founded *National Review* magazine but also gave birth to Young Americans for Freedom (founded at the Buckley estate) and later to the American Conservative Union. Accordingly, if Buckley took the lead on an issue, the vast majority of those in the conservative movement took notice and many, if not most, followed his lead.

Buckley's only blind spot was his early racial outlook, which undoubtedly was influenced by his parent's multigenerational southern heritage (Texas and Louisiana). This resulted not only in his coming late to support for black rights but also in his early support for segregation.[35] Buckley not only failed to support the Civil Rights Act of 1964; in 1961, he wrote derisively about attacks on the Freedom Riders[36] who went into the South in support of the civil rights movement. However, by the late 1960s Buckley came around and eventually expressed his regret for not supporting the 1964 Civil Right Act.[37] In 1969 he wrote an article for *Look* magazine suggesting presciently that a black American might be elected president within a decade, providing the sort of validation to black Americans that the election of John F. Kennedy provided for Catholic Americans.[38]

As one essayist wrote, *"Integration and black progress were welcomed [by National Review] when they were the result of private actions like the boycotts of segregated buses or lunch counters, which Buckley judged 'wholly defensible' and 'wholly commendable.'"*[39]

Nevertheless, Bill Buckley and the conservative movement he led did not support the civil rights movement led by Dr. Martin Luther King, Jr. An explanation of this failing is discussed in an essay by William Voegeli titled "Civil Rights and the Conservative Movement"[40]: *"On the questions where the movements [conservative and civil rights] confronted each other directly the simplest judgement is that King was right and Buckley was wrong."*[41]

Fortunately, although Buckley was indeed the undisputed leader of the conservative movement, many of those who followed him were not in lockstep with him on the issue of civil rights. In fact, one or more young conservatives approached Buckley in the early 1960s asking why conservatives should not support the civil rights movement.[42] Buckley argued against support on the basis of the argument that to do so would damage federalism as established by the Founders, violate the Constitution, and encourage the growth of big government. That argument, however, completely ignored the Fifteenth Amendment to the U.S. Constitution, which specifically guarantees the right of every American to vote. Although the civil rights struggle of the 1960s was not limited to voting, there can be no argument that the right to vote was a legitimate constitutional issue. Nevertheless, by and large, Buckley's opposition to the civil rights movement caused conservative leaders and his followers to remain silent as black Americans struggled to gain their full rights as American citizens. That silence not only was wrong, it understandably damaged the relationship of conservatives with black Americans to this day.

It is accurate to say that *"Buckley stood outside of the conservative Republican tradition of defending black civil rights."*[43] In fact, it was conservatives within the Republican Party who for decades had led the fight for civil rights over opposition from Democrats. For example, it was Republicans who fought for and passed the Civil Rights Act of 1875,[44] and it was conservative Republicans who fought to outlaw lynching as far back as 1922.[45] They also opposed poll taxes.[46] *"In 1947, the Republican-controlled Senate, headed by Robert Taft, refused to seat notorious racist Theodore Bilbo (D–MS) because of intimidation of black voters in the 1946 election."*[47] It was conservative Republican Majority Leader William Knowland who fought Democrats South and North to pass civil rights acts in 1956 (failed) and 1957 (succeeded). And of course it was conservative Republicans such as Everett Dirksen who led the successful fight to pass the Civil Rights Act of 1964.

The point is that early on Bill Buckley was out of step with the conservative political leadership in Congress when it came to civil rights for black Americans, and unfortunately he led many conservatives astray. It was a moral failure that conservatives did not unite behind the struggle for civil rights. Understandably, it broke the long-standing bond of trust that had existed between Republicans and black Americans since the time of Lincoln. In breaking that bond of trust, Republicans shattered any hope of winning over a large portion of the black vote in subsequent elections. It was tragic for black Americans, who saw the enactment of policies by liberal Democrats that resulted in the dissolution of the black family[48] and a welfare system that trapped too many black Americans in multigenerational poverty.

The fundamental question is: Why should black Americans trust conservatives when at one of the most crucial moments in the history of their struggle for freedom, conservatives declined to lift their voices or hands in support of full rights for black Americans? Black Americans at that time were risking their lives and sometimes giving them to acquire what was acknowledged in the Declaration of Independence, "that all men are created equal, that they are endowed by their Creator with certain unalienable Rights, that among these are Life, Liberty and the pursuit of Happiness." Instead, at a most critical moment in American history, black Americans were greeted by the conservative movement with silence. There were no speeches by conservative leaders outside of Congress supporting the civil rights movement. There were no articles in conservative publications supporting the struggle of black Americans for their freedom.[49] There were no programs or projects supporting civil rights for black Americans by conservative organizations. And although Young Americans for Freedom held a gigantic rally in Madison Square Garden for "Victory Over Communism,"[50] there was no similar rally by YAF for the rights of black Americans in the South. As former *New Guard* editor Arnold Steinberg wrote, *"The conservative movement failed in civil rights because it rejected its own premise—voluntary action to end racial discrimination."*[51]

Apparently, too many conservatives were blind to the obvious fact that right in their own country a struggle was being waged for the rights of black citizens that deserved their full support. What many conservatives still fail to understand is that the civil rights struggle of that era was *the* battle that counts more than anything else with black Americans, and understandably so. It was a watershed moment in black American history. Yet sadly, no chorus of conservative movement voices was lifted in support of those valiant fellow Americans.

Today black Americans might say to conservatives, "If you were passionate about the freedom of Czechoslovakians, Latvians,

Poles, Romanians, Ukrainians, and all the other people enslaved behind the Iron Curtain yet remained silent in the struggle of fellow Americans to gain their own freedom, why should I even give you the time of day? Such silence speaks volumes about your true commitment to individual freedom. At best it betrays your blindness to the struggle in your own country for basic human rights. At worst, it implies a rejection of the very words of the Declaration of Independence and a racist indifference to the second-class status of your fellow American citizens. How could you ignore your fellow citizens who had for more than a century been denied their full citizenship rights and the respect they deserved as equals under the law and in the eyes of God?" And, they might add, "Simply supporting issues that benefit black Americans today does not wipe away the memory of your silent betrayal in the midst of the most crucial battle for the individual freedom of fellow Americans since the American Civil War. Without one acknowledgment of 'I was wrong, please forgive me' you now want me to trust you and vote for you. So if you really want to understand why black Americans don't vote for you, there's your answer. We still do not trust you."

Some conservatives will protest that they personally intervened when a black friend was discriminated against during the civil rights period. Others will argue that there was nothing they could do because the rule of law and the Constitution kept them from supporting the 1964 Civil Rights Act. Or they will say their hands were tied because Dr. Martin Luther King, Jr., accepted the support of those on the far left, even communists.

Those black Americans whose votes are sought by conservatives might say, "Black brothers and sisters were dying, Mississippi was on fire, and we were in a life and death struggle for our freedom, and you expect us to apologize for accepting the help of anyone who would give it? You wouldn't give us your support, so we took support from any person or organization who would help us. And you can come up with any excuse you want for your nonsupport—the

Constitution, federalism, the rule of law—we don't care. We waited a hundred years for full rights as American citizens, and we were unwilling to wait any longer. You weren't there for us when we needed you; why should we be there for you now?"

That's exactly how Vernon's mother, Stella Pecot, felt. She risked her life to register black voters. In 1944, Stella was president of the local chapter of the Southern Negro Youth Congress while attending Dillard University in New Orleans. While there she tried to register to vote but was repeatedly turned down. For instance, when asked to give her age, she had to state the year, month, and day of her birth. Then she would be asked a question about the Constitution, and even though she answered it correctly, she was told that her answer was wrong.

One weekend, Stella went to her home in Franklin and asked her mother about the candidates on the ballot that year. Her mother replied that she could not vote and so she did not pay any attention to the candidates running. Stella then asked her mother whether the black high school principal, the two black physicians, or the black pharmacist who owned a drugstore could vote. No, her mother said. They were not allowed to vote; no black person was allowed to vote.

Being the strong person she was, Stella went to visit those prominent men, and by the time she returned home, Mr. Simmy (a black man who owned a nearby bar and sweets shop) had been there, urging her mother to get Stella out of town before she was lynched! Stella left immediately because she knew that such threats had to be taken seriously in Louisiana in 1944. Later, she learned from her son, Vernon, that the Southern Negro Youth Congress that she was associated with in college was listed by the FBI as a communist front organization. When she heard that, she just shrugged. The truth is, Vernon's mother cared only about making it possible for black Americans to vote. She was fighting for her freedom and that of her children yet unborn, and she could not have cared less where her support came from.

Conservatives may nod their heads and say that they understand why Stella Pecot was willing to work unknowingly for a communist front organization that was attempting to register black voters. But some would quickly caution that if you destroy the rule of law in your quest for full citizenship rights, specifically including the right to vote, you will do great damage to the U.S. Constitution and to the principle of federalism. That argument, however, ignores the specific language of the Fifteenth Amendment to the Constitution that was passed in 1870: "The right of citizens of the United States to vote shall not be denied or abridged by the United States or by any State on account of race, color, or previous condition of servitude." Moreover, having been a part of the conservative movement for more than fifty years, I [Bruce] can honestly tell you that if my passionate conservative friends had been born into a black family in the deep South in the 1930s or 1940s, they would have been leading the charge for full citizenship rights for themselves and their fellow black Americans during the height of civil rights activity in the South during the 1950s and 1960s. They would not have been patient, and they would not have been deterred by any other considerations. I doubt that you, dear reader, would have been deterred either.

Yet today some of those conservative friends still defend Goldwater's no vote on the 1964 Civil Rights Act. However, I doubt that they would defend their silence and lack of support for the civil rights struggle of the 1950s and 1960s. Like me, they know that they were wrong in not supporting the efforts of black Americans to claim their full rights as American citizens. It's time to talk about it. It's time to admit that we were wrong, very wrong.

The following exchange between Bruce and Lee Edwards,[52] the recognized historian of the modern conservative movement, who was present at the Buckley estate in Sharon, Connecticut, at the founding of Young Americans for Freedom, got right to the bottom line:

Bruce: Young Americans for Freedom ignored the idea of freedom for black people.

Lee: Well, Bruce, I think we stand accused.

Bruce: I do, too.

Lee: I think we stand accused, indicted, and convicted, all three.

Bruce: I agree.

Lee: And, I think that we paid a terrible price for that. And Bruce, we're still paying a price all these years later, 50 years later.

A very strong argument can be made that the policies conservatives support today are truly beneficial to black Americans and, in contrast, the policies of those on the left, in the Democratic Party, are detrimental to the success and well-being of black Americans. However, in lieu of black Americans and conservatives having a relationship built on trust, that argument undoubtedly will fall on deaf ears, especially in the older black community.

There's a second reason most black Americans choose not to vote for conservative Republican candidates. Many years ago, after the 1964 election, conservatives and Republicans made a conscious political decision not to spend time or money communicating with black voters. They gave up on getting black support. They threw in the towel. This only exacerbated the estrangement between black Americans and conservative Republicans.

Meanwhile, Democrats consciously increased their communication with black voters, whose numbers continued to expand. Because black voters heard only one side of the story for more than 50 years, the views and policies of Republicans and conservatives were severely distorted in their eyes. Year after year, black Americans were told that all conservatives were racists and that the Republican Party was racist. Those communications not only served to strengthen the ties of black Americans with the Democratic Party but also heightened their distrust of Republicans. The Democrats' outrageous, dishonest, and disgusting ads over black media depicting Republicans and conservatives as racist completely decimated the Republican/conservative brand. Those attack ads were designed to make sure the Democrats could consistently win 90 percent or more of the black vote. And that's exactly what happened for more than half a century. Of course, as the number of black voters continued to increase, the black vote made winning elections much easier for the Democrats.

Donald Trump was the first Republican candidate for president in recent history to go directly to black voters, and it paid off. In fact, Trump made a direct, if somewhat blunt appeal to black voters in 2016, saying, *"What in the hell do you have to lose?"*[53] In addition to that, Trump and super PACs such as the 2016 Committee and Americas PAC made direct appeals to black Americans over black radio stations and via social media. Those appeals were based primarily on a meta-study conducted by the late Richard Nadler that provided substantiation of the effectiveness of such appeals.

As a result, as was alluded to earlier, according to a poll taken just four days before the 2016 presidential election, 21 percent of black voters in Pennsylvania (more than 140,000) voted for Donald Trump for president.[54] This breakthrough support level not only provided much more than Trump's margin of victory in that crucial state, it also proved that conservatives and Republican candidates can win a large share of the black vote because they are natural allies.

Perhaps even more encouraging is the steady exodus of black Americans from the ranks of the Democratic Party to the Republican Party. An August 15, 2019, Zogby Analytics survey[55] indicated that 28 percent of black voters approve of the performance of President Trump and are likely to vote for him. In reality, the actual percentage of black voters inclined to support

President Trump in 2020 may be substantially higher as conservative black Americans are often targets of liberal shaming and thus are reluctant to tell a pollster that they will be voting for Donald Trump. Although this movement of black Americans to Trump may not yet be a flood, the tide has turned, and a historic opportunity awaits Donald Trump in 2020.

Equally important, a number of these escapees, such as Candace Owens of Turning Point USA and the recording star Kanye West, have not done so quietly, nor have they acted defensively. They have refused to be shamed into silence by the Democrats and the left-leaning news media. Instead, like their forbearers in the civil rights movement of the 1950s and 1960s, they have gone on offense, courageously exposing the fact that the policies of today's Democratic Party are often completely foreign to the values and aspirations of black Americans.

Similarly, Donald Trump has opened new avenues of communication with black Americans, reminding them that the policies the Democrats advocate not only undermine black economic success but also run counter to the moral and social values to which they subscribe. Trump's alliance with black pastors and young black leaders is strong and growing.

Remember, if a typical Republican candidate for president receives just 20 percent of the black vote, it becomes nearly impossible for a Democratic candidate to win, as Donald Trump proved in 2016 in Pennsylvania. If the Republican candidate wins 25 percent of the black vote, the Democratic candidate has a near zero chance of winning an election. There is no reason to believe that Donald Trump can't reach that magic number in the key swing states in 2020. That is what this book is really about: Donald Trump winning 20 percent or even 25 percent of the black vote in 2020, which would assure him of a resounding victory. To do this, Trump doesn't have to reinvent the wheel; he can learn from Franklin Roosevelt, who flipped 70 years of black allegiance to the Republican Party in just 4 years.

CHAPTER 3

Again in 2020?

Within the space of two presidential elections, 1932 to 1936, black Americans en masse left the party of Lincoln to support Franklin D. Roosevelt. How did it happen so quickly and so totally? It's an amazing story with powerful lessons for Donald Trump in 2020. In 1932 Herbert Hoover won the black vote overwhelmingly. Considering that most enfranchised black Americans were living in northern big cities at that time, this table provides a good picture of black voting that year. Of course, black Americans in the South were generally denied voting rights.

Presidential Vote in Major American Cities 1932[56]

City	% Republican	% Democratic
Chicago	75.1	21.0
Cincinnati	71.2	28.8
Cleveland	82.0	17.3
Detroit	67.0	31.0
Knoxville	70.2	29.8
New York	46.0	50.8
Philadelphia	70.5	26.7
Pittsburgh	56.2	41.3

Nevertheless, black American dissatisfaction with the Republican Party began in 1932 and was led by Robert Lee Vann, editor of the *Pittsburgh Courier*, a widely read black newspaper. Vann had been a prominent black leader in the Republican Party since the 1920s, but he *"had had enough"*[57] by 1932. He saw in Franklin Roosevelt someone who was willing to pay attention to the needs of black Americans. Vann was passionate, and he persuaded one of Roosevelt's top politicos, James Farley, to make an outreach to black Americans in Pennsylvania.

Remember, the Democratic Party of 1932 was still the party of Jim Crow[58] segregation and the Democrats' enforcers, the Ku Klux Klan. Moreover, Roosevelt had to count on support from progressive segregationists in the South. The fact is that Roosevelt would not have received as many black votes as he did in 1932 if President Herbert Hoover, considered to be a very progressive Republican, had not gone out of his way to alienate black leaders: *"Throughout his tenure Hoover charted a course for his party which alienated many black voters."*[59]

Hoover and the Republicans simply took black Americans for granted since they had been completely loyal since the Civil War. Black Americans, however, were understandably becoming impatient with Republicans, as they are with today's Democrats. At the Republican National Convention in 1932, black leaders and the NAACP pushed for *"a forthright denunciation in the convention platform of discrimination, lynching, and the lily white movement,"*[60] but instead the GOP inserted a plank in its platform expressing friendship with black Americans. Although Hoover easily won the black vote in 1932, this cavalier attitude and lack of serious attention to the rights and lives of black Americans set the stage for what happened in the 1936 presidential election. *"John Hope Franklin, the dean of black historians, argues convincingly that Hoover was largely responsible for laying the foundation for disaffection of blacks from the Republican Party during his presidency."*[61]

The attitude and policies of Hoover and the national Republican Party opened the door to the mass exodus of black Americans from the Republican Party, and that's exactly what happened. The Gallup Poll showed Roosevelt winning an astonishing 76 percent of the black vote in 1936.[62] To put this in perspective, black Americans were denied the right to vote in the South, where the majority of them lived. However, they could vote in the North, and their numbers there had been growing since the Great Migration of black Americans began around 1910. By the end of 1919, more than 1 million black Americans had left the South for better opportunities, safety, and more freedom in the North and West. This exodus included Mallie Robinson who left Cairo, Georgia, in 1920 with her children, including her baby, Jackie, for Pasadena, California. Jackie Robinson, of course, was later to break the color barrier in major league baseball, a truly historic event.

The fact that Franklin Roosevelt went from losing the black vote nationwide in 1932 to 76 percent support from black voters in 1936[63] is astounding, but that it occurred in just a four-year span is even more shocking. Considering the deep emotional ties of black Americans to Abraham Lincoln and the Republican Party for more than 70 years, this shift in support probably was the most rapid transfer of political support in American history. How did it happen?

The GOP exacerbated its growing rift with black Americans at its 1936 national convention by refusing a seat at their press tables to the *Pittsburgh Courier*,[64] one of the most important black newspapers in the nation. In contrast, the Democrats *"seated ten black delegates and twenty-two alternates from twelve states."*[65] This was the first time that any national convention of the Democratic Party had had black delegates or alternates. But that was just the beginning. Black reporters were seated with white reporters, a black pastor gave an invocation, and both FDR and John Nance Garner received seconding speeches by black Americans.[66]

Time and *Newsweek* magazines took note of the fact that this was the first time that either party actively solicited black voters.[67] The finally awakened Republicans announced *"plans for the most intensive campaign among the Negro race ever waged,"*[68] and the Democrats undertook *"elaborate and unprecedented efforts to woo the colored gentry away from the G.O.P."*[69] In addition, both parties advertised in black newspapers and magazines, distributed literature, and created movie shorts promoting their candidates.[70] For the first time, both political parties took black voters seriously. The battle was joined, but it was not sullied by charges of racism against either party. The Democrats got off to a fast start.

Immediately after his inauguration in 1933, an effort was undertaken by Roosevelt and his political team to reach out and recruit black Americans to the New Deal.[71] Of course, from the beginning, Franklin Roosevelt's interest in black Americans was primarily political. As Roosevelt's official biographer, Arthur Schlesinger, Jr., put it, Roosevelt *"was fairly conventional in his racial attitudes."*[72] Indeed, while a state senator in New York, he wrote in the margin of one of his speeches *"story of a N-word,"* and as assistant secretary of the Navy, he was instrumental in making toilets segregated in the *"State, War, and Navy Department Building."*[73]

When it came to matters of legislation, FDR regularly subjugated the interest of black Americans to the need for support from the powerful bloc of southern Democrats in Congress. As a result, most New Deal programs discriminated against the interest of black Americans. For instance, the National Recovery Act (NRA) gave white Americans first choice of jobs and, distressingly, provided for lower pay scales for black Americans.[74] Similarly, the Agricultural Adjustment Act was supposed to aid more than 2 million sharecroppers by providing cash and raising the price of farming commodities.[75] In reality, however, relief *"was monopolized and inequitably distributed by landlords, who frequently reduced the acreage of cotton by evicting their black tenant farmers.*"[76]

Perhaps most shocking of all, in 1937 Roosevelt appointed Hugo Black of Alabama, a member of the Ku Klux Klan, as an Associate Justice of the U.S. Supreme Court.[77] This was Roosevelt's first nomination to the Court. He later claimed that he was unaware of Black's KKK connection,[78] although even if that is true, it is unlikely he was unaware of Black's extreme racial animus toward black Americans.

Clearly, Roosevelt's outreach to black Americans was focused on supporting Roosevelt, not the Democratic Party. If the focus had been on the Democratic Party, it surely would have failed, for the Democratic Party in 1933, the year of Roosevelt's inauguration, was heavily influenced by and identified with Jim Crow[79] Democrats from the South. Understandably, it had no credibility with blacks who were fleeing that region. For obvious reasons, Roosevelt walked a political tightrope, appealing to black voters while trying not to alienate his powerful white segregationist base.

Roosevelt's strategy worked. Ironically, it wasn't that the Roosevelt administration did anything significant for black Americans between 1932 and 1936; rather, it was the fact that Roosevelt no longer was ignoring black Americans and their votes. To be sure, the close relationship of first lady Eleanor Roosevelt to black leaders such as Mary McLeod Bethune, a frequent visitor to the White House and later the highest-level black appointee in the Roosevelt administration, publicly illustrated FDR's interest in black Americans.

The intent was to obtain black support for Roosevelt and then, when it was politically feasible, transfer that support to the Democratic Party. Confirmation of the success of this strategy is provided by the fact that by 1948, for the first time, more blacks thought of themselves as Democrats than as Republicans.[80] Of course, it helped that earlier that year Truman had issued an order desegregating the military and issued an executive order ending racial bias in federal hiring.[81] Nevertheless, it took from 1936 until 1948, a span of 12 years, for black support to be transferred from Franklin Roosevelt to the Democratic Party. In 1948, 56 percent of blacks identified as Democrats,[82] up from a tie with the Republicans of 40 percent in 1944.

Until FDR, no other Democratic president had made such an overt and intentional outreach to black Americans, just as no Republican candidate for president had made such a concerted and direct appeal to black Americans as Donald Trump has. FDR's successful outreach to black voters in 1936 was truly a turning point in American politics and was the reason for the dramatic and rapid transfer of political support of black Americans from the Republicans to Franklin D. Roosevelt in 1936 and beyond.

After 1936, black Americans no longer were attached to the party of Lincoln; now they were attached to Franklin D. Roosevelt. It wasn't that the steps were dramatic; it was the fact that there was a concerted outreach to black Americans that included giving black political leaders a seat at the table in the Democratic Party.

The Great Migration of black Americans from the South that began with American entry into World War I made the black vote in the North a significant factor in national elections. It was the power of the black vote that Roosevelt sought to help secure his reelection in 1936 and the years beyond. It has paid huge dividends for the Democratic Party. Once black Americans won their voting rights in the South in 1965, the value and power of the black vote increased dramatically. In 1936, Democratic candidates across the nation, except in the South, followed the lead of Roosevelt, ultimately securing a strong black allegiance to the Democratic Party at every level. As the years passed, this marriage of black Americans to the Democratic Party that began with Roosevelt took on new meaning and importance in winning elections at the city, state, and national levels. In fact, without it, countless Democratic candidates for office, including those running for the White House, would have failed.

In some ways it was an odd marriage, but in other ways it made sense. It was odd in that very little was done by the Democrats to improve the lot of black Americans during the Roosevelt years. A heavily Democratic-dominated Congress did not pass civil rights legislation, did not outlaw lynching, and did not outlaw poll taxes or even so-called literacy tests for voting in the South. It took a Republican President, Dwight Eisenhower, and a Republican-controlled Congress to pass the first civil rights legislation since Reconstruction, the Civil Rights Act of 1957.

Nevertheless, it was Roosevelt who made the first move toward acknowledging the equality of black Americans with white Americans, even if his motivation was political. But motivation was not of primary concern to black Americans; it was results that counted. Although it may have been political considerations that drove the Democratic Party to appeal to black voters, it was a critical first step in recognition, respect, and acceptance that put black Americans on the road to equality and full rights as American citizens.

Following the example of the Roosevelt administration, succeeding Democratic administrations used the same game plan, building close personal relationships with black leaders, appointing black men and women to high positions in government, and promising and often delivering government programs to benefit that constituency. Regulations were passed, executive orders were issued, the promises grew larger, and with each new directive, program, and appointment the bond of loyalty was sealed even more tightly between the Democratic Party and the black community. Sadly, some of the programs ended up being destructive to the black family and made it more difficult to achieve economic success. For the Republicans, it was too late; the bond of trust had been broken. The allegiance of black Americans to the Democratic Party was a fait accompli.

Ultimately, in the twentieth century, with the unintentional help of the Republicans, Democrats reinforced their hold on the black vote, consistently winning as much as 90 percent or more of that growing political bloc. This put them in the enviable position of being able to automatically count on this expanding voting base to support candidates at the national, state, and local levels. However, this reliance has also caused Democrats to take black support for granted. Unfortunately, they see black Americans only as a source of votes, not as true equals or as a community that deserves high-quality schools, safe neighborhoods, and a sure pathway to economic growth.

Regrettably, the Democratic Party has become a Democratic plantation where black Americans are expected to toe the line and even vote for Democrats whose values are contrary to their beliefs. Recently, this has caused restlessness among black Americans. This unease, reinforced by the support of policies and programs that hurt poor black Americans, has provided an opening for Donald Trump to turn the tables on the Democrats. Yes, there is an opportunity for Donald Trump to do in 2020 what Franklin Roosevelt did in 1936, but with the liberal monopoly of the news media, it's going to be very, very difficult even though it is long overdue.

CHAPTER 4

A Liberal Nightmare

Movement conservatives definitely owe black Americans a heartfelt apology for not actively supporting the civil rights movement of the 1950s and 1960s. But frankly, this failure by the conservative movement is overshadowed by the historical fact that the segregation of black Americans from white Americans was initiated by leaders of the American liberal/progressive movement. It was undoubtedly the worst kind of social engineering ever orchestrated by the liberal/progressive movement in America.

According to award-winning author David Southern, *"All but a tiny handful of white progressive thinkers subscribed to either biological or cultural racism, or some combination thereof."*[83] Young progressive intellectuals in college during the early years of the twentieth century didn't just read books and materials attacking capitalism, they also *"read racist tracts"*[84] based on flawed *"psychology, sociology, genetics, [and] eugenics"*[85] that posited the inferiority of black Americans.

That's right: Segregation wasn't something that just happened; it sprang from the progressive belief in the inferiority of the black race. On the basis of that false belief, progressives proceeded to enact laws segregating black Americans from white Americans. Nor was the implementation of this evil progressive idea limited to the South, where segregation exhibited its worst traits. Regrettably, in one form or another, it spread across the entire nation.[86] In fact, by the early 1920s even the liberal state of *"Oregon was so firmly in the grasp of the hooded nightriders [KKK] that the governor admitted they controlled the state."*[87] Yet to hear today's mainstream media and the Democrats tell it, it was conservatives who were responsible for segregation. That is simply a calculated lie designed to cover up progressive culpability for foisting segregation on our nation. Today proud heirs of progressive thought have the audacity to argue that wearing a MAGA hat is equivalent to wearing a Ku Klux Klan hood.[88] But of course every member of the KKK that existed after the Civil War and was reconstituted during the Woodrow Wilson era[89] was a Democrat. Moreover, every KKK member to sit in the U.S. House of Representatives and the U.S. Senate was a Democrat.[90] In fact, the KKK under segregation was *"the domestic terrorism arm of the Democratic Party."*[91]

Perhaps not so ironically, Antifa[92] serves the same role today that the Klan served many years ago. Antifa riots, destroys property, attacks Trump supporters and conservative speakers,[93] and then mysteriously disappears, just as the Klan did. The only difference is that the Klan members hid their identity by wearing masks and white robes, whereas Antifa militants dress head to toe in black, wearing masks to hide their identity. Just as the progressives of another era refused to denounce the Klan, not one prominent liberal has denounced the violent antics of Antifa. Progressive Robert Byrd (Democratic Senate majority and minority leader) was *"a recruiter for the Klan"* and rose *"to the title of Kleagle and Exalted Cyclops"*[94] of the Klan in the 1930s. Similarly, liberal Dartmouth professor Mark Bray not only supports Antifa but defends its violence as being *"ethically reasonable."*[95]

For eight years Barack Obama actively worked to enrage Americans and divide them by race, sex, age, and income level, but that didn't deter the *Washington Post* from running a headline that read *"Trump's Era of Hate."*[96] This is the oldest trick of the left:

to blame Donald Trump and conservatives for what they themselves are guilty of. Today's Democratic Party owns racism, just as it owned segregation and slavery.

"[T]he Democrats have never admitted their racist history, never taken responsibility for what they did, never apologized for it."[97] Many lies have been told to cover up the racist policies of the American progressive movement and the Democratic Party, but the long history of the Democrats and their racist actions and policies has been well documented even though this research has been ignored by the mainstream media. As Dinesh D'Souza wrote, *"The Democratic Party's racism after the Civil War was preceded by the Democratic Party's defense of slavery."*[98]

Lest the reader think that statement is too harsh, for nearly 100 years Democrats across the nation enthusiastically celebrated Andrew Jackson Day. Jackson was the hero of Democrats from coast to coast and border to border. Only recently have the Democrats quietly shelved these annual celebrations to take the public eye off their racist past. Jackson, the founder of today's Democratic Party, was not only a notoriously brutal slave owner but also the instigator of the infamous Trail of Tears[99] march of death that forcibly removed American Indians from historic lands they had been awarded under treaty.

As was noted previously, Democrats also hold the distinction of being the only slaveholders in America. Not one Republican has ever been identified as a slaveholder, and that's not surprising. The Republican Party was formed in 1854 in Wisconsin by abolitionists. They wanted to block the extension of slavery in any new states coming into the Union. Democrats opposed this because they knew that it ultimately would mean the end of slavery in America. Once the number of free states—states in which slavery was banned—sufficiently exceeded the number of slave states and their populations, the free state congressmen and senators would have the votes needed to pass a constitutional amendment banning slavery. It was not just southern Democrats who wanted to bring in more slave states: *"The Northern Democrats were in bed with the South on slavery."*[100] About a hundred years later, northern Democrats (including Senator John F. Kennedy[101]) joined with southern Democrats to vote against the Civil Rights Act of 1956. Contrary to lies told by the Democrats, all the civil rights acts received strong support from conservative Republicans. We now know that progressives intentionally instituted segregation, but what was the political circumstance that made segregation possible?

"Beginning in 1890, a wave of [voter] disfranchisement swept through Dixie, as every southern state enacted literacy tests, poll taxes, and other restrictions making it virtually impossible for black men to vote."[102] Although the imposition of segregation didn't happen overnight, Louisiana provides a good example of what took place after 1890. By 1896, there were still 130,334 registered black voters in Louisiana, but by 1904, when the full impact of progressive restrictions on black voting were in place, that number fell to 1,342.[103]

Segregation was made possible by the end of Reconstruction in the South and the failure of a legal challenge to it in *Plessy v. Ferguson*. That case challenged the right of the state of Louisiana to force blacks to ride in separate railroad cars. The challenge reached the U.S. Supreme Court but was rejected in 1896. That opened the door to disallowing blacks' access to all public accommodations in the South. If the Civil Rights Act of 1875 had been sustained or the *Plessy v. Ferguson* ruling had gone the other way, there would have been no need for the Civil Rights Act of 1964. But these tragic misjudgments by the Court allowed progressives to force segregation on the South, and they did.

"The most progressive politicians in the South, where almost 90 percent of African Americans lived from 1900 to 1917, led campaigns for legal segregation and disfranchisement of blacks and even vowed to lead lynch mobs against black men accused of raping white women."[104] In other words, those leading the charge for the imposition of segregation weren't southern conservatives or

southern businessmen; they were southerners who were highly educated, very liberal white intellectuals. *"Racism was conceived by some as the very foundation of Southern progressivism."*[105] Among those progressives was *"Edgar Gardner Murphy, one of the most articulate and cultured of Southern progressives."*[106] Sadly, the views of southern progressives were similar to the thinking of progressives who lived outside the South.[107] *"Most progressive intellectuals in fact acquiesced in the consolidation of Jim Crow in the South."*[108] In fact, they not only acquiesced, they supported segregation across the United States.

Progressive intellectuals who orchestrated segregation were certain that science proved black Americans to be inferior to white Americans. Edward Ross, a PhD from Johns Hopkins University, wrote in 1901, *"The superiority of a race cannot be preserved without pride of blood and an uncompromising attitude toward the lower races."*[109] A longtime friend and mentor of Ross (and Woodrow Wilson), Professor Richard T. Ely, *"agreed with Edward Ross that certain races . . . were inherently inferior."*[110] Ross further *"advised progressives to discard the sentimental, religious equalitarianism of the old abolitionists and base their ideas of reform on hard science."*[111] The hard science that Ross referred to was of course not science at all; it was just an ideologically warped justification for segregation. Note that the strident demand for relying entirely on hard science sounds eerily similar to today's insistence by progressives that "settled science"[112] proves the existence of human-caused global warming. In both cases, it is not hard or settled science that reinforces their case but rather ideologically contrived "sky is falling" emotion that drives their efforts to diminish the individual freedom of American citizens. Real science that is subject to open debate and scientific peer review is the last thing progressives sought then or seek today.

The fundamental flaw of progressivism is the idea that human nature can be improved. The previously mentioned sociologist Edward Ross, a leading light of the early progressive movement and the author of more than a dozen books, *"believed that some human beings had evolved to the point that they could use their brains to . . . effect a fairer and more democratic society."*[113] The same argument is put forth by liberals today, that they have reached a higher ethical level that enables them to make better decisions than others can make. Thus Joe Biden's appraisal of Trump supporters as the *"dregs of society."*[114]

This rejection of the biblical understanding of human nature runs totally counter to the beliefs of America's Founders, who *"realized that our human nature could, and often did, pervert the plain dictates of conscience, allowing us to convince ourselves that right is wrong and wrong is right if it suits our own desires."*[115] The Founders correctly understood that humans live in a fallen state. Indeed, Washington, Adams, Jefferson, Franklin, Madison, and others expressed the essential need for virtue inspired by faith in God in order for the newly created republic to survive. Dr. Benjamin Rush, signer of the Declaration of Independence, tied it together, writing that *"the only foundation for a useful education in a republic is to be laid in Religion. Without this there can be no virtue, and without virtue there can be no liberty."*[116] Like the leaders of the French Revolution who *"rejected the Judeo-Christian notion of the fallen nature of man in exchange for the idea that he could be perfected by reason,"*[117] the progressive movement embraced the idea that they could modify human nature and create people who were ethically superior to their fellows.

Not surprisingly, *"every prominent progressive individual at the turn of the twentieth century denounced the Declaration as an old and stale way of thinking about society."*[118] In a 1907 Independence Day address, Woodrow Wilson stated that *"each generation must form its own conception of what liberty is"* and later said, *"Mr. Jefferson and his colleagues in the Continental Congress prescribed [the meaning of liberty]. . . for no generations but their own."*[119] Wilson emphasized this point by saying, *"We are not bound to adhere to the doctrines held by the signers of the Declaration of Independence, we are as free as they were to make and unmake governments."*[120] Contrary to the understanding of the Founders, *"Wilson believed that the human condition improves as history marches forward."*[121] Wilson's mentor at Johns Hopkins University, Richard T. Ely, liked to quote from T. H. Green, a noted English neo-Hegelian, writing, *"'True liberty' does not consist in 'negative' freedom, in, that is, the legal freedom to make decisions about one's own life without suffering interference from others."*[122] Similarly, in a 2001 radio interview, Barack Obama spoke of the U.S. Constitution as *"a charter of negative liberties"*[123] that fails because it does not *"say what the Federal government or State government must do on your behalf."*[124] In other words, liberty as redefined by Obama, Wilson, Ely, and the founders of the progressive movement does not mean that every citizen has the right to make his or her own decisions about how to live. Instead, it means that those who have reached a higher ethical plane have the right to use government to tell others how to live and what to think and that government should go beyond the Constitution and do things for Americans. Apparently, for today's liberals, America should not be the "land of opportunity" but rather the "land of entitlement." The ideas of Wilson, Ely, and Obama, who believe our rights are granted to us by government, stand in stark contrast to the foundational principles of the Founders and President Trump, who said it clearly: *"Our rights are not given to us by man; our rights come from our Creator."*[125]

The progressives' morally corrupt and incorrect understanding of human nature provided Wilson and other progressives with the ethical and intellectual cover they needed to tighten the grip of segregation in the South and expand it across the nation, and that's exactly what they did. Despite the Fifteenth Amendment to the U.S. Constitution guaranteeing the right to vote to black Americans, southern progressives used every means possible to circumvent the Constitution and deny that right to black Americans.

Sadly, the damage to black Americans wasn't limited to the South. Once Wilson was elected president in 1910, those progressives also *"pursued policies that harmed the other 10 percent of blacks who live north of the Mason-Dixon Line."*[126] *"The early years of the twentieth century saw increasing hostility toward blacks in the North as well as in the South. More and more, blacks faced segregation in or exclusion from northern restaurants, hotels, and theaters."*[127] Of course, this spread of segregation was led by liberal progressives, North and South.

This made things much worse for black Americans. For example, in 1900 the southern states spent about twice as much per white student as they did per black student. After liberal progressive "reforms" were imposed, the amount of money spent on black education *declined* sharply, falling to just 13 percent of the amount spent on white students.[128] By any honest account, Woodrow Wilson's election in 1910 was disastrous for many generations of black Americans.

Yet even today liberals such as Hillary Clinton, who received the Woodrow Wilson Award for Public Service,[129] speak Wilson's name in reverence. The reality is that Woodrow Wilson, the first American president to openly attack both the Declaration of Independence and the U.S. Constitution,[130] is revered by progressives who have nothing but contempt for America's Founders.[131] Considering the rancid racism of Wilson, it is odd that in the last few years those on the left, such as Hillary Clinton, have stopped describing themselves as liberals and instead have started to call themselves progressives in honor of Woodrow Wilson.

Segregation wasn't the only evil consequence of the idea that human nature can be improved, nor was it the only social engineering scheme of the progressive movement. Progressives' belief in the so-called science of eugenics was also disastrous for black Americans. Eugenics champion Margaret Sanger, who founded Planned Parenthood, repeatedly expressed the desire to rid America of undesirables through her "Negro Project"[132] and thus to create *"a race of thoroughbreds."*[133] For liberals, eugenics too was *"based on cutting-edge science."*[134] The damage it did and continues to do to black Americans is enormous. Although liberals today steer clear of using the word *eugenics*, its corrupt theory lives on for those who support Planned Parenthood and its targeting of black babies for abortion. If you have any doubt about the fact that Planned Parenthood targets black babies for abortion, look at this misleading 2017 tweet from that organization: *"If you're a Black woman in America, it's statistically safer to have an abortion than to carry a pregnancy to term or give birth."*[135] Or consider that an Ohio state representative *"Janine Boyd, a Democrat, proposed Amendment 0291, which provides an exception for black mothers"*[136] to the bill outlawing an abortion if there is a heartbeat. Apparently, Democrat *"Boyd thought it important that blacks continued to be exterminated, even though white babies were protected by the new law."*[137] By the way, the so-called heartbeat law was passed by the Republican-controlled Ohio state legislature and signed into law by the Republican governor Mike DeWine over opposition from Democrats such as Janine Boyd.

"In her 1922 book 'Pivot of Civilization' she [Sanger] unabashedly called for the extirpation of 'weeds . . . overrunning the human garden' . . . and for the sterilization of 'genetically inferior races.'"[138] If you can't guess who Margaret Sanger was referring to, she wrote in her autobiography, *"I accepted an invitation to talk to the women's branch of the Ku Klux Klan."*[139]

Nevertheless, when Hillary Clinton received the 2009 Margaret Sanger Award given by Planned Parenthood, she said, *"I admire Margaret Sanger enormously, her courage, her tenacity, her vision . . . I am really in awe of her."*[140] Clinton and other liberals reveal that they still harbor a eugenics mindset when they refer to the supporters of Donald Trump as "deplorables."[141]

Sanger was not only a leader in the eugenics movement; she also had close ties to Hitler's Nazi Party through her friend and fellow eugenics supporter Ernst Rudin. Sanger published a 1933 article by Rudin in *The Birth Control Review* (the forerunner to the *Planned Parenthood Review*) titled "Eugenic Sterilization: An Urgent Need."[142] Rudin was at that time Hitler's director of genetic sterilization and was a founder of the National Socialist German Workers' Party (Nazi). *"Before the Nazis gave eugenics a bad name, it was a kind of secular religion in America."*[143] Eventually, progressives dropped the use of the word *eugenics* when it became too closely tied to Hitler's Nazi Party.

Although there were liberal/progressive Republicans such as Wisconsin Governor Robert La Follette who were enamored of eugenics, no conservative Republicans bought into this evil idea. Of course, Sanger's malevolent ideas still poison the thinking of Democrats. For example, in 2019 Virginia's liberal Democrat governor Ralph Northam made it clear in a radio interview that he believes that infanticide, the killing of a newborn baby, can be justified.[144] In response to Northam's advocacy of infanticide, Donald Trump spoke out strongly: *"Do you remember when I said Hillary Clinton was willing to rip the baby out of the womb? That's what it is, that's what they're doing, it's terrible."*[145] Clearly, the view of today's Democrats that babies do not have the right to "life, liberty, and the pursuit of happiness" strengthens the need for the kinds of judges President Trump has been appointing and reinforces the reason he must be reelected in 2020.

CHAPTER 5

Twenty-First-Century Democrats

Since Trump supporters and Donald Trump are smeared as racists nearly every day by the news media, let's take a look at the race record of today's Democrats who claim to be champions of black Americans.

Democrats claim that black babies are not specifically targeted for abortion, but the facts suggest otherwise. Although black women make up just 14 percent of the female population, they account for 36 percent of all abortions.[146] Sadly, there are 474 abortions for every 1,000 live births of black babies in the United States.[147] In fact, as of June 2015, 19 million black babies had been aborted since 1973.[148] These are gruesome numbers. They might make Margaret Sanger and Governor Ralph Northam glad, but they are tragic for the babies, for the black community, and for America. How and why is this happening? It is happening because Democrats and liberal Republicans make sure that Planned Parenthood receives hundreds of millions of your tax dollars each year.[149] In return, these Washington, D.C., politicians receive huge political contributions from Planned Parenthood. It's no wonder Democrats support abortion and the federal funding of Planned Parenthood.

According to one report, *"79% of Planned Parenthood's surgical abortion facilities are strategically located within walking distance of African and/or Hispanic communities."*[150] Abortion is not only a human tragedy and a callous destruction of human life, it also robs the black community of its very future. If those babies had not been aborted, the black population would be 36 percent larger than it is today.[151]

Would a friend who really cares about you support an organization that targets your baby for abortion? Of course not. But Democrats fight hard to provide federal funds for Planned Parenthood. As a result, in the 2018 election cycle alone, Planned Parenthood spent more than $4 million, almost all of which went to pro-abortion Democrat candidates.[152] Between 1990 and 2018, of the $7.9 million donated by Planned Parenthood and its affiliate organizations to political candidates, $7,663,909 (96.8 percent) went to Democrats.[153]

Like most people with common sense, Donald Trump knows that it takes at least two things to succeed in life. One is character, and the other is a good education. Why, then, do elected Democrats, black and white, oppose school choice, including the educational vouchers that have been proved to be effective in lifting the poor out of poverty and that are supported by a vast majority of black Americans?[154] The answer is that they have been bought off. Affiliates of the National Education Association (NEA), the nation's largest teachers union, spend huge sums each year to fight against charter schools and school choice. They also make donations to Democratic candidates nationally and in the states to elect legislators who will be friendly to them and carry water for them. Nearly all of the $18,128,105 the NEA spent in the 2018 election cycle went to support Democratic candidates.[155] Even black Democrats find the price of opposing the teachers union on school choice too high to pay. The NEA fights school choice for two reasons: first to protect jobs and second to make sure that they control what students are taught in school. The NEA is one of the most radical left unions in America.

The dirty little secret is that although many prominent Democrats send their children to private schools, they deny black parents that choice. Clearly, Democrats don't think that black children are as deserving of a high-quality education as their own children are. In addition, it is obvious that Democrats put a higher value on the money that comes from the NEA than they do on the lives of black children. Although Barack and Michelle Obama sent their children to a private school, one of the first things Obama did after becoming president was cancel the Washington, D.C., school choice program. Even liberal commentator Juan Williams called his decision to end the program *"Obama's outrageous sin against our kids."*[156]

Not surprisingly, the alarm bells sounded when the Democrats recaptured control of the U.S. House of Representatives in 2018, putting federal support for high-performance choice schools across the nation (that had been proposed by the Trump administration) in jeopardy.[157] The fact is that when it comes to black children getting a good education, Democrats and the National Education Association are the enemy of a quality education for poor black students, whereas conservatives and Donald Trump are their friend.

Nothing has changed with the Democratic Party. As slaveholders, they callously broke up families. As segregationists, they forced black people to sit at the back of the bus and kept black Americans from voting. Today, liberal Democrats keep black children from getting the education they need to escape poverty, the kind of good education that comes from the school choice programs promoted by President Trump.

Whereas Donald Trump wants to build a wall to make America secure, leading Democrats want to tear down the existing wall.[158] They favor allowing millions of unskilled poor men and women, not to mention MS-13 gang members and sex traffickers, to enter the United States illegally. How does this adversely affect black Americans? More than half of black Americans are economically in the middle class, another quarter are among the working poor, and the remaining 21.2 percent are in poverty[159] and depend entirely on government assistance. Those black Americans who are among the working poor want to move up to the middle class, and the poor want to escape poverty by getting a job. But flooding our nation with millions of poor people from other countries makes it even harder for a poor black person to get a job and move up the ladder of success. Not only do poor black folks lose jobs, those who have escaped poverty see their wages driven down by illegal immigrants. Those who favor unlimited immigration are supporting an idea that hurts not only poor black Americans but also black bricklayers, bank tellers, teachers, and others in the public sector because they don't speak Spanish. In short, an open borders policy is in reality a dagger at the heart of the black middle class and all black Americans endeavoring to climb the economic ladder of success.

Although Donald Trump's policies have brought down the price of gasoline and heating fuel, Obama and other Democrats are on record expressing a desire *"to boost the price of gasoline to the levels in Europe,"*[160] where gasoline prices have reached as much as $8.00 per gallon.[161] This doesn't affect the wealthy, and although it does hurt the middle class, it is absolutely devastating for the poor and the working poor. Why? For wealthy people, the additional cost of gas and fuel is a small percentage of their income and does not affect the way they live. For those in the middle class it is a significant share, but it is something they can bear. However, for people at the bottom rung of the wage scale or for those receiving government support, it is devastating because the cost of gas, heating fuel, and energy devours a huge percentage of their monthly income.

"The National Black Chamber of Commerce estimate[d] that the [Obama] Clean Power Plan [would] lead to 7 million job losses for African Americans and 12 million lost for Hispanics, with the poverty rate increasing by more than 23% and 26%, respectively. Another study by the Pacific Research Institute found that the rule would increase home energy bills for African Americans

by $410 a year."[162] Access to low-cost energy is always the key to prosperity in a nation, and inexpensive energy is also essential for escaping poverty and climbing the economic ladder. That's one reason President Trump has worked hard and been successful in dramatically lowering the cost of energy.[163] He wants to see all Americans, especially poor black Americans, prosper. Opposition to cheap fuel costs by Democrats is in opposition to poor Americans' efforts to escape poverty, especially poor black Americans.

The racist Davis–Bacon Act became law on March 31, 1931, and thanks to Democrats it is still in full force notwithstanding liberals' claims that they are friends of black Americans. This law grew out of a complaint by New York representative Robert Bacon, who complained that union workers in New York had been undercut by a bid by an Alabama contractor to build a government marine hospital on Long Island. The employees of the contractor were all black and were paid a lower wage than the union workers in New York. The Davis–Bacon Act compelled all federal contractors to pay the "prevailing" wage in that state. The American Federation of Labor, which excluded black workers at that time, immediately backed the bill. Construction was one industry in which black workers excelled at that time, but from that point forward the law effectively excluded them from working on any government jobs. Democrats still support continuation of the Davis–Bacon Act. Why? Because they count on union money to back their candidates for public office. Once again, when it comes down to a choice between more jobs for black Americans and continued financial support from unions, Democrats opt for the money.

Indisputably, the black church is the most powerful force for good in the black community, and for that reason, when it comes to moral and social issues, black Americans tend to have a very traditional viewpoint. Accordingly, among all groups—black, white, Hispanic, and Asian—black Americans are the only one that does not support same-sex marriage.[164] They align with white and Hispanic conservative evangelical Protestants on this matter.[165] In the past, when black Americans were allowed to vote on this issue, they strongly opposed homosexual marriage. In 2008, 70 percent of black Americans who cast their ballots voted in favor of a ban on homosexual marriage in California.[166] In spite of the overwhelming defeat of homosexual marriage in California, an ideologically driven liberal judge found an excuse to invalidate the election results. Even in a recent poll, less than 50 percent of churchgoing black Americans supported gay marriage.[167] Yet Democratic Party leaders and officeholders continue to ignore the wishes of black American Christians. One hopes that the constitutionalist judges being appointed by Donald Trump to the federal courts and the U.S. Supreme Court will reverse this ruling.

However, it's not only on the national or state level that Democrats work against the interest and views of black Americans. Big cities run by Democrats also make rules and regulations that hurt both black employees and black entrepreneurs. License requirements for barbershops and hair braiding and beauty salons hurt both black consumers and black entrepreneurs.[168] Not only is a financial barrier imposed that makes it harder for a new business to start up, the black consumer is required to pay more for the services he or she desires. The worst government restrictions are those which negatively affect both black entrepreneurs and black consumers.

In the case of taxicabs, a city-sanctioned monopoly effectively makes that form of transportation unavailable to poor black Americans in many, if not most, big cities, all of which are run by Democrats.[169] Typically, those already providing such services lobby city council members to impose requirements (which are as effective as poll taxes) to block the entry of black entrepreneurs into the marketplace. The pretext for such regulations is usually safety, but in reality such regulations have one purpose: to use the power of government to eliminate competition, especially low-cost competition, from black Americans. Existing cab companies want to limit competition so that they can maintain higher prices. The council members in return receive sizable contributions from the owners of the cab companies when election time rolls around. The people who lose the most are those at the bottom end of the economic ladder, often black Americans struggling to escape poverty and work their way up the ladder of success. Nevertheless, Democratic politicians always choose the money from the establishment businesses over a free marketplace that helps the poor.

Despite this Democratic war on black entrepreneurs, thanks to the economic policies of Donald Trump, *"The number of African American small business owners in the United States has increased by a staggering* 400% *in just a year."*[170]

There are other issues that adversely affect the well-being of the black community. In nearly every instance, Democrats are on the wrong side and Donald Trump and conservative Republicans are on the right side. For Democrats and their megaphones in the media, racism is only about words, but real racism is based on actions such as supporting slavery, voting against the Fifteenth Amendment granting voting rights to black Americans, instituting Jim Crow[171] segregation in the South, blocking high-quality schools for black children, targeting black babies for abortion, and creating barriers to economic success such as artificially raising energy prices. Today, by any reasonable standard, the policies and practices of liberal progressive Democrats cannot be characterized any other way than as being racist.

Racism has been and is the hallmark of the Democratic Party throughout its history. The very last thing liberal Democrats want is to have Trump expose their duplicity and win over black voters in 2020. But there is even more to this story, as we shall see.

CHAPTER 6

Lyndon Johnson

When Donald Trump and all Republicans and conservatives are figuratively tarred and feathered almost every day by the news media as racists, it turns reality on its head. But to understand how this lie got started, you have to go back to Lyndon Johnson, congressman, senator, vice president, and president. Johnson was willing to do literally anything to win.[172] He, more than any other American politician, turned winning into a blood sport, and his legacy is in great part responsible for the disgusting and disgraceful attacks on President Donald Trump. Johnson was the first Democrat to brand Republicans as racist, a label that is placed on Donald Trump supporters today. If you want to know why being a conservative or a Republican automatically makes you a racist according to the left, this is a story you will want to hear.

Who was Lyndon Johnson? *"He was deceitful and proud of it."*[173] If he had to lie, he lied. If he had to steal votes, he stole votes.[174] If he had to bribe a senator with pork or with women, he did it with no compunctions or regrets. *"He seemed to feel himself bound by nothing."*[175] He had to win every fight, and win he did, once saying, *"I do understand power, whatever else may be said about me. I know where to look for it, and how to use it."*[176] Isn't this a good description of today's Democrats, who seek power at any cost? They brainwash students with lies about America's

Founders, and they use every opportunity to smear Republicans, conservatives, and especially Trump supporters as racist or even white supremacist. Of course they know it is a lie, just as Johnson knew he was lying. Today's radical Democrats don't hate Donald Trump because they believe he is a racist; they hate him because they hate anyone who stands in their way of gaining power. Like Johnson, they love power and want total power over your life. This chapter and the next contrast the "racist" Barry Goldwater and the civil rights "champion" Lyndon Johnson.

Johnson and Goldwater were men of the same generation and had gotten to know each other when they served in the U.S. Senate. Both were from the Southwest. Johnson was born in 1908, and Goldwater in 1909. One man undertook innumerable personal acts to end racial discrimination and would never tolerate a racist comment in his presence. The other man repeatedly voted against laws to abolish lynching, poll taxes, and so-called literacy tests and used the "N-word" throughout his life, from his childhood through his tenure in the highest levels of government.

Johnson was and is hailed as a great man. *"Lyndon Baines Johnson was the greatest champion that black Americans . . . had in the White House, the greatest champion they had in all the halls of government. With the single exception of Lincoln, he was the greatest champion with a white skin that they had in the history of the Republic."*[177] In contrast, during the 1964 campaign—and even today—Goldwater was reviled as a racist for his vote against the 1964 Civil Rights Act. But in both cases the truth is much more complicated than that, as we shall see.

Lyndon Johnson was elected to the U.S. House of Representatives in 1936 and to the Senate in 1948. On the day of his announcement in Austin, Texas, that he was running for the U.S. Senate, Johnson minced no words regarding civil rights for black Americans. In his speech he *"condemned proposals for the equal opportunity laws"* and *"stormed against civil rights bills."*[178] Not only did Lyndon win the election, but after serving just four years in the Senate he became minority leader, and when the Democrats gained a majority, he became the youngest majority leader in the history of the United States. It was unquestionably an incredible political accomplishment.

Lyndon Johnson wasn't just opposed to civil rights for black Americans; he used racist, condescending words when talking with black Americans such as Robert Parker. Parker was a native of Wichita Falls, Texas, who with the help of Johnson had secured a patronage job as a postman in Washington, D.C. In return for Johnson's help in securing the job, Parker was expected to serve as an unpaid bartender at Johnson's parties during the 1940s and 1950s. He also filled in as a chauffeur when Johnson's regular chauffeur wasn't available. For *"years"* according to Parker, Lyndon Johnson called me *"N-word, or Chief never by my name."* One day, however, when Parker was serving as chauffeur, Johnson asked him, *"Chief, does it bother you when people don't call you by name?"* Parker was understandably cautious in answering, but he said, *"Well, sir, I do wonder. My name is Robert Parker."* That was not the answer Johnson wanted or expected, because he exploded in rage, shouting, *"Let me tell you one thing, N-word. As long as you are black, and you're gonna be black till the day you die, no one's gonna call you by your goddamn name. So no matter what you are called, N-word, you just let it roll off your back like water, and you'll make it. Just pretend you're a goddamn piece of furniture."*[179] Is this the quintessential Lyndon Johnson, or did Johnson have a road to Damascus change of heart upon becoming president of the United States?

During his time in the Senate, Johnson was closely allied with the Southern Caucus that was controlled by Richard Russell. Yet after succeeding in crushing the civil rights bill of 1956, Johnson changed his strategy on the 1957 civil rights bill. Lyndon had a very important political reason for a change in strategy: He was seriously considering a run for the White House (he did run and barely lost to John F. Kennedy at the 1960 national convention of the Democratic Party in Los Angeles). With his astute political finger in the wind, Johnson understood that he couldn't win a national race running as a segregationist. He was a shrewd politician and realized that when it came to civil rights for black Americans, the political winds were changing. Regardless of his personal views on race, Johnson the politician was determined to be on the winning side of the civil rights debate.

In 1956 Dwight Eisenhower again beat Adlai Stevenson in a landslide (neither candidate hinted or suggested that the other was a racist). The reelection of Dwight Eisenhower with strong black support worried Johnson. Johnson, of course, was right about the historic opportunity Republicans had in 1960 to regain the black support they had lost under FDR. Republican action on civil rights in the South and advocacy of civil rights legislation presented a direct threat to the Democratic Party, and Lyndon knew it. During the 1956 election campaign, NAACP lobbyist Clarence Mitchell, Jr., campaigned hard for the Republicans, traveling to key states and speaking to black voters across the nation.[180] By winning more than 39 percent of the black vote in 1956,[181] Eisenhower had set the stage for a big GOP comeback with black voters in the 1960 presidential election. With black Americans moving their way, the Republicans were determined to pass civil rights legislation with real teeth in it when the new Congress convened in 1957. Their plan was to give the U.S. Department of Justice the power to enforce the voting rights of black Americans in the South, and they believed they had the votes to make it happen.

With that in mind, Lyndon Johnson decided to take a different tack on the Civil Rights Act of 1957. He went to his friends in the Southern Caucus with a number of arguments: "*The times were changing, he told them. . . . Civil rights was a big issue and it was going to get bigger—and we look bad on that issue. The Republicans had decided to do anything they had to do to win the N-word vote. The Republicans were making civil rights a party issue—their issue.*

It's a tough issue for the Democrats. It's hurting us. Look what happened in the last election."[182] After softening the southern senators up, he engineered a compromise that would help him with a White House bid without alienating his fellow segregationist Democrats. It was a political tightrope act, but Lyndon pulled it off by outmaneuvering Republican Senate Majority Leader Bill Knowland. This enabled Lyndon to vote for the Civil Rights Act of 1957. It was politically possible for him to do that because he successfully gutted the bill by changing the enforcement mechanism from being the U.S. Department of Justice to local juries in the South. This change secured his continued good standing with the Southern Caucus. They knew and Lyndon knew that there wasn't a single southern jury that would vote to enforce any aspect of the Civil Rights Act of 1957.

Instead of the act having the teeth that Knowland and the Republicans sought, it could more accurately be described as toothless thanks to Johnson's changes. It enabled the Democrats to hold on to the black vote nationally and at the same time allowed southern Democrats to continue their suppression of the black vote in their home states. It was a cynical yet politically successful strategy that did not benefit black Americans in the way the Republican version of bill would have.

So why is Lyndon Johnson hailed as second only to Lincoln in securing rights for black Americans? The answer is that once President John Kennedy was assassinated and Johnson became president, Lyndon Johnson championed and signed the Civil Rights Act of 1964 and the Voting Rights Act of 1965 into law.[183] Did his support for civil rights legislation signal that Johnson felt genuine remorse for his previous racism and bigotry? Did he have a true epiphany and sincerely regret his past opposition to full freedom, voting rights, and civil rights for black Americans?

Indeed, as President Johnson proclaimed, *"I never had any bigotry in me. My daddy wouldn't let me."*[184] Most reporters took Johnson at his word, but his record before becoming president made it clear that this statement was simply not true, as even a friendly biographer, Robert Caro, acknowledged.[185] But that still does not answer the question whether Lyndon Johnson regretted and repented of his previous opposition to basic freedom and civil rights for black Americans. There are countless stories throughout history of men and women who, like the Apostle Paul, made a total about-face and in contrition repented of their sins and changed their ways. Was that what happened in the case of Lyndon Johnson?

How President Johnson acted and what he said *after* signing important civil rights legislation should give us a clue whether his championship of civil rights for black Americans was a cynical political calculation or a genuine change of heart. Fortunately we have a somewhat extensive record of Johnson's attitude and language (as well as that of immediate family members) regarding black Americans after he became President of the United States. These individuals were spoken to directly by Johnson or by family members or were overheard by them.

During a flight on Air Force One, President Johnson discussed with two presumably southern Democratic governors why his proposed 1965 Voting Rights Bill was so important to him. It turns out the president was overheard by Air Force One purser Robert MacMillan, a black man. According to MacMillan, Johnson said, *"I'll have them N-words voting Democratic for two hundred years."* In MacMillan's view, *"That was the reason he was pushing the bill, not because he wanted equality for everyone. It was strictly a political ploy for the Democratic Party. He was phony from the word go."*[186] But MacMillan wasn't the only person to overhear a candid President Johnson talking about black Americans.

Associated Press photographer Steve Stibbens was on assignment, taking photographs for a feature story at the Johnson Ranch during the Johnson presidency, when he accidentally heard the president talking to ranch hands over a radio telephone. Apparently, Stibbens heard the "N-word" used by Johnson over and over. Stibbens said, *"I was so shocked—I couldn't believe what I was hearing—I mean, this was the great civil rights president."*[187]

On another occasion in 1967, Texas state official Larry Temple met with President Johnson in the White House, where they talked about possible black nominees to the U.S. Supreme Court. Johnson was intent on nominating only someone who would help him and the Democrats politically. He said with all the crudeness of a dyed-in-the-wool racist, *"When I appoint a N-word to the bench, I want everyone to know he's a N-word."*[188]

In 1968, before Johnson announced that he would not run for another term, Hubert Humphrey talked with him about the challenge for the presidential nomination that the president was facing from Bobby Kennedy. Humphrey told Johnson he was sure that blacks wouldn't abandon him for Kennedy after the president had backed and signed the 1964 Civil Rights Act. Johnson replied, *"Hubie, after all these years, you still don't know a damn thing about N-words. What the hell does a N-word know about loyalty?"*[189]

Finally, there was the encounter that the Air Force One purser Robert MacMillan had with Luci Johnson, the president's youngest daughter, when the airplane made a brief stopover in Florida. According to MacMillan, Luci was very angry. She said to him, *"Damm you. You go find my N-word right now!"* When MacMillan played dumb, she screamed, *"Find my N-word!"* Then she started to slap him, to which he responded, *"Miss Johnson, I don't think that would be a good idea."* Finally, Luci said, *"Dammit. I'll find him myself."*[190] Clearly, Luci had learned to use this disgusting word because at least one of her parents used it regularly.

Of course, it wasn't just that Lyndon Johnson was a racist. The fact is, he was immoral in virtually every respect, as the following story indicates. A well-known Washington journalist had a rather shocking encounter with Johnson. This widely respected journalist was a man of good character who reverenced the tradition and importance of the White House. He was understandably flattered when he received an invitation to visit the Johnson Ranch in Texas to interview President Johnson.

Upon arriving at the ranch, this gentleman was ushered into a room with the president. They exchanged pleasantries and then sat down. Soon a pretty young girl entered the room and proceeded to sit on one of Johnson's widespread legs. As if that wasn't outrageous enough, Johnson proceeded to reach around and put his hand over her breast. Soon the first lady entered the room and sat on Johnson's other leg, and Johnson did the same thing with Lady Bird. The journalist was shocked and later told two close friends that when this happened, he couldn't breathe because he was so stunned at the president's debauched behavior.[191] This episode is just one of many stories about Johnson's coarse, rude, immoral behavior.

Does it seem reasonable to conclude that a debauched lifelong racist like Lyndon Johnson suddenly had a dramatic change of heart on the race issue just when it happened to be politically beneficial to him and the Democratic Party to do so? Or would it seem more logical to conclude that a man of such low moral character who had multiple affairs,[192] who made no secret of the fact that he stole votes in elections,[193] and who often made cruel fun of his wife[194] was cynical enough to flip-flop on civil rights purely for political gain?

The point is not just that Lyndon Johnson was a disgusting racist but rather that in the 1964 race, for the very first time, a Republican candidate for president and all his followers were smeared by Johnson, the Democrats, and the complicit news media as racists. And it worked so well that the Democrats adopted it as a permanent fixture of every subsequent campaign, be it for president, governor, senator, congressional representative, or any other office. For more than half a century this has been the game plan of the Democratic Party, and it has been crassly reinforced by the news media. How ironic is it that the party that fights against quality schools for poor black Americans, targets their babies for abortion, and otherwise keeps black Americans from realizing the American dream accuses Republicans and conservatives of being racists? But what about Goldwater? Was he the disgusting racist he was portrayed to be?

CHAPTER 7

Barry Goldwater

To fully understand the challenge facing Donald Trump in his attempt to win over black voters in 2020, it's critical to understand who Barry Goldwater was and what really happened when he ran for president in 1964. It's a lesson that must be learned if black and white Americans are to unite to save the nation from the ravages of the radicals who have captured the Democratic Party.

Barry Goldwater was the first conservative to win the Republican nomination for president since Calvin Coolidge, and although the election result was a political disaster, it set the table for Ronald Reagan's landslide presidential victory in 1980. Of course, that result was not apparent at the time. In fact, in 1964 it was impossible to determine whether Goldwater's nomination was truly a long-term turn to the right for the Republican Party. Most seasoned observers at the time were skeptical that it was indeed a turning point in the history of the GOP.[195] As one writer put it years later,

> The election proved to be a watershed moment in American political history—but not in the way most contemporaries viewed it. Democrat Lyndon Johnson trounced Republican Barry Goldwater in a huge landslide. To most observers at the time, liberalism rode triumphant and conservatism crumbled,

> with some even talking of the demise of the Republican Party. But it was not to be, as the liberal wave crashed almost immediately and conservatives came to dominate a resurgent Republican Party in the late twentieth century.[196]

One man who was certain that the Republican Party was finished as a result of the 1964 election results was James Reston of the *New York Times*, who gloated, *"Barry Goldwater not only lost the presidential election yesterday but the conservative cause as well. He has wrecked his party for a long time to* come."[197] Reston could not have been more wrong.

We now know that with the nomination of Barry Goldwater, the control of the GOP by the eastern liberal establishment was gone for good. Liberal control was replaced by a more conservative populist rule by the party's grass roots, whose base was primarily in the Midwest, the West, and to some degree the South. This change in command led to a political realignment that resulted in dramatic victories for Richard Nixon in 1968 and 1972, Ronald Reagan in 1980 and 1984, George H. W. Bush in 1988, George W. Bush in 2000 and 2004, and Donald Trump in 2016. But if that's true, why did Goldwater lose so badly in 1964?

Not only was 1964 a turning point in control of the GOP, it also was a turning point in the mainstream media striving to report the news objectively. In 1964, for the first time, the media dropped all pretense of objectivity and replaced it with advocacy journalism. They became openly partisan in their attacks on Goldwater and Republicans in general. Indeed, the media attacks on Goldwater, as well as those instigated by the Johnson campaign, were among the nastiest in the history of American politics, even by today's standards. It can be fairly said that they were as dishonest and unfair as the attacks on Donald Trump more than five decades later.

Headlines from the campaign include the following: *"Roy Wilkins Charges Goldwater 'Out of Munich Beer Halls,'" "Gov. Brown Says Barry Has 'the Stench of Fascism,'"* and *"Goldwater*

Victory to End U.S. Elections."[198] Throughout the 1964 campaign, major newspapers ran stories that included quotes such as *"Senator Goldwater has become a rallying point for all the racists in America,"*[199] *"In this crucial period, the election of Goldwater as President would be a catastrophe. The whole free world would disintegrate for lack of confidence,"*[200] and *"The Cow Palace at times rang with echoes from the Munich Beer Hall. . . . The danger is that Goldwater may be the precursor of an American totalitarianism."*[201]

Not to be outdone, Lyndon Johnson's vice-presidential running mate, Hubert Humphrey, said that *"what we are talking about in this election is life itself, the future of the planet, the salvation of the species."*[202] Finally, there was *"Election of Senator Barry Goldwater could pave the way for a fascist take-over of America."*[203] The Goldwater campaign marked the beginning of the end of responsible journalism in America when it came to covering conservative candidates.

On top of that were the ill feelings of the 1964 presidential candidates toward each other. For his part, Johnson had long hated Goldwater because he could not be bought. He couldn't bribe Goldwater with the promise of a new dam in Arizona or any other kind of pork barrel spending. Goldwater wouldn't play ball, and that frustrated Johnson, whose modus operandi as Senate majority leader was the manipulation of others to do his will. Accordingly, Goldwater and Johnson never got along in the Senate or after Johnson became president. Barry Goldwater's votes and principles were not for sale.

However, what should we believe about Barry Goldwater and civil rights? Was he the racist he was portrayed to be by the media at that time? Was he a man of low character like Johnson? No, he wasn't, even according the *Washington Post*'s obituary, in which that liberal newspaper wrote that Barry Goldwater was a man whose *"reputation for personal integrity was unblemished."*[204] That was high praise from a paper that rarely had a good word to say about Goldwater while he was alive.

Young Barry Goldwater planned to follow in his father's footsteps, working in the family business, but while he was attending the University of Arizona in 1929, his father died suddenly of a heart attack. That forced Barry to drop out of college at 20 years of age and immediately begin learning the family business at the Goldwaters' store in Phoenix. By 1937, he had become president of the Goldwater firm, which was by then a local chain of popular and *"trend setting"*[205] department stores.

Not long after becoming the head of the company, Barry Goldwater integrated the store for both black customers and black employees.[206] It was a bold move, especially in Phoenix, which was at that time a distinctly southern town, but it wasn't the last bold move by this fair-minded man. Also in the 1940s, Barry Goldwater and his friend Harry Rosenzweig spearheaded the successful movement to desegregate the lunch counters in Phoenix.[207] After Barry left active duty with the Army Air Corps in World War II, he received a request in 1945 from the Democratic governor, Sidney Osborn, to organize the Arizona Air National Guard. It was in this role that he desegregated that organization more than two years before President Truman issued an executive order to integrate all the U.S. armed forces.[208]

Goldwater's first entry into politics was in early 1947 when the Democratic mayor of Phoenix, Ray Bussey, appointed a citizens committee to revise the city charter.[209] Bussey's goal was ending the corruption that had been flourishing in Phoenix, especially prostitution. Goldwater and other leading citizens were asked to serve on the committee. The charter was changed and modernized, but the corruption continued, and in 1949 Goldwater was persuaded to run for the Phoenix City Council to help clean up the dishonesty. Goldwater led the ticket, receiving strong support on the south side of the city, where blacks and Mexican Americans were concentrated. Those minorities trusted Goldwater, and their trust was justified when, as a member of the Phoenix City Council, he endorsed and financially backed the NAACP campaign for the integration of Phoenix public schools.[210] Goldwater and the new council members also succeeded in cleaning up the rampant corruption in Phoenix.

In 1952, Goldwater decided to toss his hat into the ring and run against the Democratic Senate majority leader, Ernest McFarland. It was a long-shot run considering the fact that nearly 85 percent of the voters in Arizona were registered as Democrats, but Goldwater won in a squeaker.[211] Of course, it didn't hurt that war hero Dwight Eisenhower carried the state in a huge landslide victory. Ike won by more than 43,000 votes, compared with coattail-riding Goldwater, who won by less than 6,500.[212]

One of the key elements of Goldwater's campaign was his support for full citizenship rights for American Indians.[213] He had traveled to all the reservations in Arizona, visiting with ordinary men and women as well as their leaders. As a U.S. senator, he became their champion, as he had been as a businessman.

Coming to Washington, D.C., in 1953 as the senator-elect from Arizona, he brought his legislative assistant, Kathrine Maxwell, with him. But when Maxwell, a young black woman, went to the Senate cafeteria to eat lunch, she was told that the cafeteria was only for white employees. Incensed and offended by this insulting affront to his legislative assistant, Goldwater immediately contacted the cafeteria manager and let him know in no uncertain terms that from that day forward not only would Kathrine Maxwell be allowed to eat at the Senate cafeteria, so would all the other black employees of the Senate. Furthermore, Goldwater warned the cafeteria manager that if he refused, Goldwater would hold a news conference the next morning that was sure to make the front page of the *Washington Post*, condemning the practice of segregation in the Senate cafeteria. From that day forward, the Senate cafeteria was fully integrated thanks to the personal intervention of Barry Goldwater, who did so without any fanfare or personal horn blowing.[214]

This action by Goldwater was characteristic of his passion for justice and fairness when it came to race or any other matter. But as far as Goldwater was concerned, he just did what was right, and he didn't want any publicity for simply doing the right thing. It was for that reason he would not allow Lee Edwards, who handled public relations for the Goldwater for president campaign in 1964, to use this story. Being honorable, decent, and fair was important to Barry; that was what good people were supposed to do.

Goldwater's action on behalf of Kathrine Maxwell was just one instance of a lifelong pattern of support he provided for black Americans struggling for equal rights. In 1952, as a citizen of Arizona, he donated $200 to the Arizona NAACP to hasten integration of the public schools.[215] A contribution of $200 may not seem like much today, but it is equivalent to nearly $1,900 in 2019 dollars.[216] It was no small sum, but Goldwater's financial support of the civil rights movement didn't stop there. He financially backed the Phoenix Urban League, personally covering their operating deficit for two years in a row.[217] He also made it a point to introduce the president of the Phoenix Urban League, Junius Bowman, to the most important and well-heeled citizens in Phoenix, giving Bowman a means of raising additional funds for the civil rights organization.[218]

In appreciation of Goldwater's longtime generous support, in 1991 the Phoenix Urban League honored him with its Humanitarian Award *"for fifty years of loyal service to the Phoenix Urban League."*[219] Barry Goldwater was a member of both the Phoenix and Tucson chapters of the NAACP for many years. As early biographer Edwin McDowell observed, *"Few men not deliberately courting minority bloc votes have expressed their sympathy for [black Americans]—verbally and through action—more often than Goldwater."*[220]

Barry Goldwater had a long and clear record of working for and supporting civil rights for black Americans in Arizona and as a U.S. senator, yet in the 1964 presidential campaign his detractors successfully painted him as a racist. How did that happen?

The answer is his vote against the Civil Rights Act of 1964. It was a terrible mistake that his detractors in the media and his opponent in the election, Lyndon Johnson, seized upon to tar and feather him as a racist. What irony: Lyndon Johnson, a name-calling racist throughout his lifetime, was able to label Barry Goldwater, a longtime civil rights advocate, a racist! Because the smear was so successful, the media and the Democrats from that time forward have called every Republican candidate for public office a racist. In doing this, the Democrats and their friends in the media successfully destroyed the Republican brand with black Americans. For that reason, even today, the one-third of black Americans who are conservative and agree with Republicans on all the issues still overwhelmingly vote for liberal Democrats who oppose the very things they stand for. Until Donald Trump, black Americans simply did not trust any Republican.

But why did Goldwater cast his vote against the Civil Rights Act of 1964? He had voted for the 1957 and 1960 civil rights acts, and in 1963 he offered four amendments to the Youth Employment Act, which outlawed discrimination by race, color, creed, or national origin.[221] He was totally committed to civil rights for black Americans, as his personal record testifies. He gave full-throated support to the voting rights of black Americans under the Fifteenth Amendment to the U.S. Constitution and was in favor of the 1965 Voting Rights Act[222] (he was not at that time a U.S. senator). Why, then, did he not vote for the Civil Rights Act of 1964?

From the beginning, Goldwater wanted to vote for the 1964 Civil Rights Act.[223] However, Bill Baroody, Sr., who had Goldwater's ear at the time, strongly urged him to seek out the legal opinion of a young Yale law professor, Robert Bork. Goldwater followed Baroody's advice, and Bork submitted a 75-page opinion that Goldwater thoroughly digested.[224] It was Bork's conclusion that the public accommodations provisions of the Civil Rights Act of 1964 were unconstitutional, but Goldwater was not satisfied. He still wanted to vote for the bill.

Perhaps another constitutional lawyer would come to a different conclusion, he thought. Goldwater contacted his longtime friend and confidant, Denison Kitchel, to ask for his evaluation of the Bork opinion. Kitchel, a Phoenix attorney and an authority on the U.S. Constitution, then turned to a bright young member of his firm, future Chief Justice of the U.S. Supreme Court William Rehnquist, and asked him to review the Bork opinion. Rehnquist read Bork's opinion and then provided Kitchel with a 15-page summary in which he concurred with Bork's finding that the Civil Rights Act of 1964 was unconstitutional. Kitchel then provided the supporting Rehnquist summary to Goldwater.[225]

The opinions of Bork and Rehnquist put Goldwater in a very difficult position. Barry wanted to vote for the Civil Rights Act of 1964, but he revered the Constitution. He had taken an oath to uphold the Constitution and took that oath seriously. Goldwater reluctantly concluded that he was left with no choice but to vote against the act even though he strongly supported civil rights, including access to all public accommodations, for black Americans. He was fully aware of the fact that in voting no he probably was sealing his fate in the 1964 presidential election. History proved Goldwater's assumption to be true.

Years later, Goldwater lamented his vote against the Civil Rights Act of 1964 not for political reasons but for moral reasons.[226] He hated discrimination of any kind, and he especially detested segregation and the denial of the voting rights that were guaranteed to black Americans under the Fifteenth Amendment to the Constitution. He was totally sympathetic with the civil rights cause. In fact, when Goldwater spoke at Phillips Academy just three months before the historic march on Washington at which Dr. Martin Luther King, Jr., gave his famous "I Have a Dream" speech, he said simply, *"If I were a Negro, I don't think I would be very patient."*[227] Nevertheless, Goldwater's no vote on the Civil Rights Act of 1964 did lasting damage to the Republican Party's relationship with black voters, and understandably so.

Black Americans had waited almost 200 years for the words in the Declaration of Independence to be a reality universally accepted in America: "that all men are created equal, that they are endowed by their Creator with certain unalienable rights, that among these are Life, Liberty and the pursuit of Happiness." Instead of being second-class citizens treated as inferior to white Americans, they wanted to be truly free and equal under the law and in society, using public services whenever and wherever they wanted, eating and staying where they wanted, and not being segregated from society in any regard. *"A country simply does not work when any American is denied the use of a public restroom, or can't buy a cup of coffee wherever he wants."*[228] To black Americans and all fair-minded individuals, the Civil Rights Act of 1964 was a historic opportunity to fully secure the rights of black Americans once and for all. Logically, anyone who voted against the act was considered to be an enemy of their long, hard, dangerous struggle for freedom and equal rights.

Clearly, Goldwater meant no harm. His civil rights activism over many decades proved where his heart was on the matter of equal rights for all Americans. He wasn't a racist like Johnson; instead, he had long advocated for equal rights for black Americans. His respect for the U.S. Constitution was admirable, but there was a higher law than the Constitution, and discrimination, hatred, mistreatment, and segregation violated that higher law.

Despite his sterling personal record on civil rights, Goldwater was labeled a racist, and so were all Republicans and conservatives. His no vote on the Civil Rights Act of 1964 destroyed any hope of winning a sizable share of the black vote, as both Eisenhower and Nixon had received in 1956 and 1960, respectively. It also alienated black Americans from voting for any Republican candidate for office at any level. Black trust of Republicans and conservatives was shattered, and the break appeared to be irreparable. Indeed, as Goldwater biographer Lee Edwards described it, *"Because the leader of the conservative movement voted against civil rights legislation at a defining moment in American history . . . conservatives have been branded by most blacks as racists ever since.*"[229]

The break with black voters was so complete and total that it persuaded Republicans and Republican consultants to abandon seeking black support at the polls. This giant mistake gave the Democrats a virtual death lock on the black vote, not only providing the margin of victory in many successive elections but also causing black Americans to be saddled with Democratic policies that hinder them from climbing the ladder of economic success. As we shall see, it has been to the advantage of Democrats then and now to make as many black Americans as possible dependent on the government for their survival, thus allowing them to be manipulated by cynical Democratic politicians in the mold of Lyndon Johnson.

For the first time in American history the Democratic candidate for president, Lyndon Johnson, labeled his Republican opponent, Barry Goldwater, as a racist. How ironic that a vile racist like Lyndon Johnson was able to dishonestly label a man who had for decades personally championed the rights of black Americans as a racist. But the lie worked so well that it became the permanent modus operandi of the Democratic Party in every subsequent election. Perhaps, however, truth has overcome the lie, leading to the collapse of the Democrat grip on the black vote in 2020.

As black Americans see their wages rise and the general prosperity of the black community improve, many are thinking of doing the previously unthinkable: voting for Donald Trump in 2020. Black Americans, like all Americans, want to see their country safe and prosperous, just as Donald Trump does. They have seen him take action to protect America, and they have seen their paychecks grow thanks to his policies. Perhaps the political dawn is breaking for Donald Trump and the Republican Party with twenty-first-century black Americans.

CHAPTER 8

Civil Rights Pioneers

Although Barry Goldwater's personal record in standing up for the civil rights of black Americans was enviable, he was not the only person on the right who supported and fought for those civil rights. His young conservative supporters were also willing to take action. At the 1963 national convention of Young Americans for Freedom in Fort Lauderdale, Florida, when a black delegate, Don Parker, a King County, New York, YAF leader, was refused the right to stay at the convention hotel, fellow members of his delegation and the national leadership of the organization threatened to walk out and cancel the event.[230] The hotel relented, and the convention continued. Black national board members, black chapter chairmen, and black members existed throughout the history of Young Americans for Freedom. Bigotry and prejudice were not tolerated in the ranks of YAF.[231]

Although they often are accused of doing so, Republicans and conservatives have never abandoned their great heritage from the first Republican president, Abraham Lincoln. They certainly can be blamed for the times they stood by and didn't act or speak up, but unlike progressive Democrats, they have no heritage of slavery, segregation, eugenics, and racism.

Dwight Eisenhower had a long and solid record promoting civil rights even before becoming president, and he didn't do it to gather votes or to bring attention to himself. As he wrote while president, *"We have been pursuing this quietly, not tub-thumping, and we have not tried to claim political credit. This is a matter of justice, not of anything else."*[232]

Ike was not a recent convert to advocating full rights for black Americans. In 1944, on the eve of the Normandy invasion, he had a three-hour discussion with Walter White, the executive secretary of the NAACP, about civil rights. After the meeting, White stated that in regard to segregation, *"Eisenhower was implacable in his opposition to that system, so we confined our discussion to the practical means of abolishing it as swiftly as possible."*[233]

In December 1944, during the Battle of the Bulge, as a German offensive late in the war threatened to drive the war back into Allied territory, General Eisenhower was in urgent need of additional troops. Without asking the Roosevelt War Department for permission, he issued a directive stating, *"The opportunity to volunteer will be extended to all soldiers without regard to color or race."*[234] Regrettably, the War Department responded immediately, demanding not only that the directive be withdrawn but that the original of the directive be destroyed.[235]

Ike did not give in, however. He went directly to the chief of staff, General George Marshall, who eventually allowed Eisenhower to place 2,500 black American volunteers in combat. By all accounts, those men performed with distinction and were received well by the white troops.[236] That encouraged Eisenhower to believe that integration of society could be achieved rapidly.

For Ike, the matter of equal rights for black Americans was not a minor issue. In fact, when his old friend Herbert Brownell visited him in Paris in March 1952 to urge him to run for president, Ike bluntly stated that if he was elected, his *"first order of business"* would be *"to eliminate discrimination against black citizens in every area under the jurisdiction of the federal government."*[237] Ike was even better than his word.

In 1954, with Ike in the White House and Republicans controlling both houses of Congress, exclusions were removed that had denied black Americans full access to Social Security and other benefits.[238] Incredibly, this was done over the objections of the Democrats. And as we know, it was Republicans who were the strongest supporters of the 1956, 1957, 1960, 1964, and 1965 civil rights bills.[239]

Eisenhower attacked discrimination across the federal government. President Truman had issued an order to desegregate the entire military in 1948,[240] but little happened until President Eisenhower turned the order into reality. Ike also appointed 65 black professionals to influential positions in the government and appointed a black ambassador to Romania.[241] He supported home rule for the District of Columbia, and in a matter of no small importance, first lady Mamie Eisenhower desegregated the White House Easter egg roll.[242]

Ike was just getting started. When the U.S. Supreme Court, led by Eisenhower appointee Earl Warren, ruled in the 1954 *Brown v. Topeka Board of Education* case that segregated schools were unconstitutional, black Americans were thrilled. But the democratic governor of Arkansas, Orval Eugene Faubus, refused to enforce the Supreme Court's ruling and allowed mobs to block black students from attending the all-white Central High School in Little Rock. Ike responded by sending the 101st Airborne to Little Rock,[243] making it possible for black students to attend that school. President Eisenhower's firm action was something the Democrats never would have dared to do, and it made black Americans realize that Ike was a man of his word. As a result, in the subsequent 1956 presidential election, Ike received more than 39 percent of the black vote.[244] But for Eisenhower, it wasn't about votes or elections; it was a matter of justice. When Eisenhower handed the baton to Vice President Nixon in 1960, the Republican Party was poised to recapture a large share of the black vote, possibly a majority, but that was not to be.

Richard Nixon was always an outspoken advocate of civil rights for black Americans even when it resulted in personal animosity against him, as it did during his days in law school at Duke University. As a law student in the early 1930s, Nixon was appalled at the way black Americans were treated in North Carolina. Though it was unheard of in the South in the 1930s, Nixon spoke up for black Americans, telling his law school classmates about his California friend William Brock,[245] a black football player at Whittier College. Nixon also made it a point to talk about black friends joining the Nixon family at meals and about his Milhous ancestors providing a safe refuge for runaway slaves during the Civil War.[246] Treating black Americans as equals who are entitled to full citizenship was part of who Richard Nixon was throughout his life.

As vice president, Nixon was sent on a monthlong tour of Africa in 1957. While in Ghana, he had a chance meeting with a skeptical Dr. Martin Luther King, Jr. They had a long talk and agreed to meet again when they returned to Washington. In April, Dr. King and his good friend and ally the Reverend Ralph Abernathy visited the vice president in his office.[247] Both were surprised by Nixon's straightforward position in support of civil rights for black Americans, specifically his commitment to passing the 1957 Civil Rights Act.

Indeed, Nixon fought hard for the bill, and when the Republicans were outmaneuvered by minority leader Lyndon Johnson, who effectively neutered the bill, Nixon was furious.[248] Nevertheless, Dr. King was grateful for the passage of the bill and sent the vice president a letter in which he wrote, *"Let me say how deeply grateful we are to you for your assiduous labor and dauntless courage in seeking to make the Civil Rights Bill a reality. This has impressed people all across the country, both Negro and white. This is certainly an expression of your devotion to the highest mandates of the moral law."*[249]

This kind letter not only pleased Nixon but gave him every reason to believe that he could win 40 percent or more of the black vote in a contest for the White House in 1960. He was further encouraged when in 1960 Martin Luther King, Sr., endorsed him in the Republican primaries.[250] The stage was set for Nixon to win a very large share of the black vote, especially if Dr. Martin Luther King, Jr., ultimately endorsed his candidacy.

It was not to happen. On October 19, 1960, Dr. King was arrested during a sit-in at an Atlanta department store and put in jail. On October 26, a state judge sentenced King to serve time in the general population of a state prison known to be very violent.[251] Because this was a direct threat to Dr. King's life, his friends reached out to both campaigns, asking each one to contact the judge to ask for his release. Nixon did not do that, knowing that because he was an attorney not involved directly in the case, it would be considered unethical for him to do so. Instead he asked U.S. Attorney General William Rogers to have the U.S. Justice Department intervene to protect Dr. King.[252] Inexplicably, President Eisenhower did not act. Meanwhile, *"In a breach of legal ethics, Robert Kennedy ended up calling the state judge"*[253] to seek Dr. King's release.

John Kennedy called Coretta King to express his concern and support, but Nixon did not. Upon hearing of the failure of Nixon to call the judge, Martin Luther King, Sr., reversed his previous support of Nixon and said, *"I've got a suitcase of votes and I'm going to take them to Mr. Kennedy and dump them in his lap."*[254] Thus ended an opportunity for Nixon and the Republican Party to recapture a large share, perhaps a majority, of the black vote. There is little doubt that Nixon's failure to make a call to the state judge and to Coretta King cost him the election. Somewhat surprisingly, however, Nixon still received 32 percent of the black vote in 1960.[255]

Richard Nixon and Dwight Eisenhower weren't exceptions to Republican support for black civil rights in the 1950s and 1960s. In every battle for civil rights it was conservative Republican Senate leaders such as Bill Knowland and Everett Dirksen who led the fight for those bills, always battling the Democrats for passage.

Although Richard Nixon was narrowly defeated by John Kennedy in 1960, he was elected president in 1968. After taking office in 1969, Nixon went to work on behalf of black Americans, who were still not enjoying their full rights as American citizens. School segregation in the South had been outlawed in 1954 in the *Brown v. Board of Education* ruling, but when Nixon took office, only 5.2 percent of black children in the South were attending desegregated schools.[256] Thanks to Nixon's efforts in 1972, just three years later, 90 percent of black children in the South were attending integrated public schools.[257] This remarkable accomplishment was little heralded by the national news media of the time and often is ignored by left-leaning historians.

Nixon signed the Voting Rights Act of 1970 and the Equal Employment Opportunity Act of 1972, both of which passed with strong Republican support. As president, Nixon doubled assistance to black-owned business enterprises, and the amazing result was that by 1974 two-thirds of the 100 largest black enterprises had been started during the Nixon administration.[258]

Ronald Reagan was of a similar mind when it came to civil rights for black Americans. In his autobiography, *An American Life*, Reagan wrote. *"My parents constantly drummed into me the importance of judging people as individuals. There was no more grievous sin at our household than a racial slur or other evidence of religious or racial intolerance."*[259]

Reagan was outspoken on the rights of black Americans while attending Eureka College. On a trip from Eureka to play a football game in his hometown of Dixon, Illinois, Reagan was, of course, required to stay with the team at a local hotel. However, when his coach tried to check the team in at the local hotel, the hotel manager informed him, *"I can take everybody but your two colored boys,"* to which the coach replied, *"Then we'll go someplace else."* The manager replied, *"No hotel in Dixon is going to take colored boys."*[260] Coach McKinzie then told the boys that everyone would be sleeping on the bus.

But Reagan offered a solution. He said, *"Mac, why don't you tell those two fellows there isn't enough room in the hotel for everybody so we'll have to break up the team; then put me and them in a cab and send us to my house."* Uncertain, the coach replied, *"You sure you want to do that?"*[261]

Reagan said yes and took the boys to his home, where he was greeted by his mother, Nelle. *"Well, come on in,"* she said, *"her eyes brightening with a warmth felt by all three of us. She was absolutely color blind when it came to racial matters; these fellows were just two of my friends. That was the way she and Jack had always raised me."*[262] Like his mother and father, Ronald Reagan was absolutely intolerant of any disparaging remark about any minority.

In the 1930s, as a play-by-play baseball announcer on radio station WHO in Des Moines, Iowa, Reagan was *"one among a handful [of announcers] in the country who opposed the banning of blacks from organized baseball."*[263] As president, Ronald Reagan carried on the tradition of Republicans since the time of Lincoln of believing in and supporting equal rights and opportunity for all to participate in and enjoy the American dream. One act of great importance was Reagan's signing of *"a 25-year extension of the Voting Rights Act."*[264]

Today Donald Trump is president. Like Reagan, Trump has lived his life free of prejudice and bias. In his multi-billion-dollar international company, black Americans and other minorities have been hired at all levels of the business. As president, Trump's economic policies have caused black unemployment levels to plunge to historic lows,[265] and for the first time in many years black wages and salaries are rising.[266] Perhaps most important of all, the poverty rate in America is today near an all-time low.[267] And as we know, President Trump is also battling misguided Democrats to provide poor black children with good schools. As was noted previously, his energy policies have driven down the price of heating oil and gasoline, which consume a disproportionate share of poor blacks' incomes. Finally, the First Step Act[268] and the proposed Second Step Act[269] will right a wrong and help nonviolent black inmates not only leave prison early but do so with the skills and knowledge needed to reenter the employment marketplace.[270]

In fact, at a meeting of the Opportunity and Revitalization Council led by Dr. Ben Carson (the secretary of HUD), the president said this new effort will *"coordinate efforts across the entire federal government to deliver jobs, investment, and growth to America's most underserved."*[271] As an example of this across-the-board approach, Secretary of Energy Rick Perry announced at the meeting that some of the prisoners released through the First Step Act will be learning how to drive big trucks for the energy industry, resulting in jobs that will pay $100,000 per year.[272] This is not just words; it is real action that will give these nonviolent offenders great jobs that will benefit themselves and their families.[273] No wonder pastor Darrell Scott said that Donald Trump is *"the most pro-black president that we've had in our lifetime."*[274] Perhaps this is the reason recent surveys show that an increasing number of black Americans support the policies of President Trump.

CHAPTER 9

Taking Action

Although Democrats reluctantly supported civil rights legislation for political gain, they were largely absent from critical civil rights battles that did not provide them with a political dividend. The courageous effort to integrate major league baseball in 1947 was one of those battles in which Democrats were nowhere to be seen.

An odd couple of Republicans did it:[275] Jackie Robinson and a *"conservative revolutionary"*[276] by the unusual name of Branch Rickey. Dr. Martin Luther King, Jr., told Larry King in a radio interview, *"I am not the founder of the civil rights movement. The founder of the civil rights movement is Jackie Robinson."*[277] This statement alone by the great civil rights leader makes it a story worth telling.

In 1947, the victorious Americans were back from World War II and everyone was working hard to make up for lost time. Nevertheless, Americans, black and white, closely followed baseball, which was then the nation's dominant professional sport. No other sport was even close. Television had not yet arrived on the scene. Professional football and professional basketball were secondary sports that received very little attention from the general public. But even as major league baseball dominated the American sports scene, it was still segregated. Black Americans were not allowed to play because of a so-called gentleman's agreement[278] dating back to 1890.

Ironically, before the gentleman's agreement, black players were commonplace in major league baseball, some playing the game until they retired.[279] And even after the agreement, in the 1930s white major leaguers, including big stars such as Dizzy Dean, barnstormed in the off-season against all-black teams.[280] In 1934, for example, the Dizzy Dean All-Stars, including his brother, Paul Dean, played a series of games against a team of Negro League all-stars that included Cool Papa Bell, Josh Gibson, Buck Leonard, and Satchel Paige. Those black and white baseball stars played in both minor league and major league stadiums, at times drawing crowds of 18,000 to 30,000 fans, black and white.[281] Interestingly, on the 1934 barnstorming tour the black baseball stars won seven out of nine games.[282] This was a win-win for both black and white players financially. Yet when the official major league season rolled around, the black baseball stars were barred from playing in the major leagues. Instead, those great baseball players and others like them played in the Negro Leagues.[283] It made no sense, it was wrong, black and white players missed out, and the fans missed out, but that's the way it was.

Black Americans fought in World War II for the freedom of those in Europe, but they were still denied their full rights as citizens back home in America. It was an inexcusable situation, and one man was determined to bring an end to it, at least in baseball. That man was Branch Rickey, then general manager and part owner of the Brooklyn Dodgers and one of the greatest innovators in baseball. It was Branch Rickey who created the baseball farm system. Well educated and intelligent, Rickey had both an undergraduate degree and a law degree. He had played in the major leagues and had served as a field manager. And although Rickey bravely took the first step by major league baseball to integrate the sport, he was modest when asked about his role, saying, *"As a matter of fact I do not deserve any recognition from anybody on the Robinson thing.*"[284] In a similarly modest fashion, Jackie Robinson gave Rickey full credit, saying that *"had it not been for you nothing would be possible."*[285] They were two committed Christians following the advice of Proverbs 27:2: *"Praise should come from another person, and not from your own mouth."*[286]

What animated the lives of both Robinson and Rickey was their Christian faith. Both were Methodists. Rickey was known for never being shy about putting his faith forward, and Robinson had faithfully taught a Sunday school class even while he was a star running back at UCLA.[287] A native of Ohio who was born in 1881, Rickey was also interested in politics. He was a rock-ribbed Republican who not only campaigned for countless Republican candidates but at one time was considered as a possible candidate for governor of Missouri.[288] Rickey didn't just give speeches; he donated, he knocked on doors, he did everything but run for office.[289] An ardent and outspoken anticommunist, Rickey once detoured to Westminster, Maryland, on a trip east to meet with Whittaker Chambers.[290] Rickey was an admirer of Chambers, who had courageously exposed a former top-level State Department official, Alger Hiss, as a Soviet spy. Chambers was a hero to Rickey, who undoubtedly had read his powerful best-selling book *Witness*.[291]

A transformational event took place in Rickey's life as a young coach of the Ohio Wesleyan University baseball team. The team had traveled to South Bend, Indiana, to play Notre Dame. However, when the team arrived at the hotel, the manager refused to provide a room for a black player, Charles Thomas. Rickey was incensed and after a lengthy discussion persuaded the hotel manager to allow Thomas to stay in a room with Rickey. Years later, Rickey wrote, *"That scene haunted me for many years, and I vowed that I would always do whatever I could to see that other Americans did not have to face the bitter humiliation that was heaped upon Charles Thomas."*[292]

Rickey took much abuse, including at a 1945 meeting of major league executives who berated him for even considering the idea of integrating baseball. According to Rickey's grandson, no one sided with Rickey; he was totally on his own.[293] But Rickey was not deterred; it was a question of right and wrong, and he knew he was on the right side. The opportunity to correct this wrong finally happened in 1947, when Rickey put Jackie Robinson on the Brooklyn Dodgers. Rickey had quietly sent out scouts to find not only a great black baseball player but also a man of good character who could stand up to the hatred and venom that was sure to come his way. When he heard from scouts about the incredible baseball skills of Jackie Robinson, Rickey exclaimed that Robinson was *"the ideal Negro star to lead the invasion of organized baseball."*[294] It is unclear whether Rickey made this statement before or after he had personally made inquiries in California about Jackie's character and faith. Regardless, when Rickey met Jackie Robinson, he knew he had found his man.

At their first meeting Rickey shocked Robinson when he told him that he wanted him to play for the Dodgers, not on another black baseball team, as Robinson had been led to believe. But first, as portrayed in the movie *42*, Rickey wanted to know if Robinson had the character and the guts *"not to fight back."*[295] He went further, telling Robinson that he couldn't fight back even when he was physically attacked or was called a *"black son of a bitch."*[296] He couldn't get mad, because if he did, it probably would kill the opportunity of other black baseball players to play in the major leagues. Rickey knew firsthand about the racism in the major leagues among players, managers, and owners. That was why he questioned Robinson long and hard about his ability to turn the other cheek, knowing the kind of hatred he was sure to face. Like the lawyer he was, Rickey made his closing statement: *"Now, can you do it? You will have to promise that for the first three years in baseball you will turn your other cheek. I know you are naturally combative. But for three years—three years—you will have to do it the only way it can be done. Three years—can you do it?"*[297]

Robinson replied in a throaty whisper, *"I've got two cheeks. Is that it?"*[298] Of course, what Branch Rickey wanted wasn't just that Jackie Robinson would have to have guts; he also offered the young ball player encouragement, saying quietly, *"God is with us in this, Jackie. You know your Bible. It's good simple Christianity for us to face realities and to recognize what we're up against."*[299]

Rickey and Robinson made their strongest connection through their common faith. It was settled that day. Jackie Robinson would be the first black American to play in major league baseball.

Rickey wisely started Robinson on the Montreal Royals, the Dodgers' triple A team. At his first news conference Robinson spoke calmly. *"Of course, I can't begin to tell you how happy I am that I am the first member of my race in organized ball,"* declared the lean, quiet 6-foot 190-pounder. *"I realize how much it means to me, to my race and to baseball. I can only say I'll do my very best to come through in every manner."*[300] Clearly, Jackie Robinson well understood the significance of his entry into the all-white major leagues.

Jackie was put in a very difficult position. Rickey told him he could not fight back; he could not answer in kind because equality and respect for the entire black community would be resting on his shoulders. As important as the battle for the integration of baseball was, Jackie Robinson was fighting for much more than that. It was a battle for equal rights and respect for all black Americans at a time when lynching in the South was not uncommon. But it was not just a fight for civil rights in the South; it was a national battle for the soul of America. It was about not only being treated equally but being respected as equal citizens of the United States.

Fortunately, Jackie Robinson, *"a man of the right,"*[301] was up to the challenge. Jackie relied on strength from God and the love of his wife, Rachel, to withstand the vitriol and even physical violence he faced.[302] He needed every bit of it. Jackie initially was treated with hostility even by most of his Dodger teammates, and he was taunted terribly by players and managers on the other teams. He stood up to unspeakable torment and harassment, always turning the other cheek, and still played great baseball. In fact, Robinson was voted rookie of the year in the National League in 1947, won the MVP award in 1949, and was a World Series champ in 1955. He received the ultimate baseball honor in July 1962 when he was inducted into the Hall of Fame, ending his career with a .311 lifetime batting average. After baseball, Robinson dedicated himself to ending discrimination in all aspects of American life. It is not surprising that the incredible stress he shouldered damaged his health and led to an early death at the age of fifty-three.

Robinson's sports achievements pale in comparison to the character and perseverance it took not only to integrate baseball but also to change the minds of those in our nation who looked down on black Americans as second-class citizens. It is not an exaggeration to say that breaking the baseball color barrier was the turning point in winning full citizenship rights and respect for black Americans. Shortly before he was assassinated in 1968, Dr. Martin Luther King, Jr., said, *"Jackie Robinson made my success possible. Without him, I would never have been able to do what I did."*[303]

Branch Rickey, the man who took the first step to integrate baseball, certainly would have agreed. He witnessed firsthand what Jackie went through. It made him all the more passionate about full rights for black Americans. As he said on repeated occasions, *"The Negro has never been really free in this country. Legally free since the Civil War yes, but not politically or socially free, and never morally free."*[304]

What Robinson and Rickey did was to challenge an entire nation to realize the sin and injustice they were guilty of by not treating black Americans as their fellow children of God. Dr. King was right: Breaking the color barrier of baseball was the beginning of the modern civil rights movement of the 1950s and 1960s. It was a battle begun by conservative Republicans, just as efforts to bring black Americans into full economic equality are today led by Republicans like Donald Trump.

CHAPTER 10

Malicious False Narrative

The malicious false narrative that Donald Trump and all conservatives and Republicans are racist is the foundation of the lie that has enabled Democrats to maintain a near monopoly on the black vote for more than 50 years. It is critical to understand this dishonest narrative and find a way to combat it for Donald Trump to win reelection in 2020.

Election after election, liberal/progressive Democrats repeatedly call conservatives and Republicans racist or even white supremacist. The "evidence" they present is based on an intentionally created false narrative. The revisionist history is that southern racists flocked to the candidacy of Barry Goldwater when he ran for president in 1964 and that the Republican Party completed the transition to being a racist party with Richard Nixon's "Southern Strategy" in his 1968 presidential campaign. This false tale was developed to cover up the long, ugly racist history of the Democratic Party that exists to this day. The goal of this concocted story is to transfer the long history of racism from the Democratic Party to the Republican Party, and with the help of a compliant news media, it has worked for more than a half a century.

The idea that all the racists moved to the Republican Party after 1964 and 1968 is simply false. After all, we now know that although Barry Goldwater failed to vote for the Civil Rights Act of

1964, his personal record was that of a man who repeatedly went out of his way to advance the civil rights of black Americans. As far as Nixon's Southern Strategy of 1968 is concerned, it was nothing more than a recognition that a New South was emerging. He realized that upwardly mobile southerners were tired of Democratic racism, the soft-on-communism approach of the Democrats, and the high-tax, big-government policies of the Democratic Party. Accordingly, this new southern generation was open to voting for a Republican candidate for president. Confirmation of Nixon's commitment to black Americans is provided by the indisputable fact that as president he did as much as or more than any other president to advance the rights of black Americans while in office.[305] Unlike Lyndon Johnson, Nixon worked hard to secure full rights for black Americans because it was the right thing to do, not because it was politically advantageous.

The single argument supporting the vicious myth that all the segregationists and racists came over to the Republican Party began with the 1964 switch of a single Democrat, Senator Strom Thurmond of South Carolina, to the Republican Party. There is no doubt that Thurmond was a racist and a segregationist. In 1948, he ran for president on the Dixiecrat ticket, a breakaway from the Democratic Party that supported the continuation of segregation. Thurmond's racism was inexcusable and disgusting, but unlike most of his southern Democratic colleagues, he was an economic conservative and a hawk on foreign policy. The Republicans could have rejected Thurmond, but they didn't.

But if that one transfer of a racist from the Democratic Party to the Republican Party makes the Republican Party racist, what about the scores of other southern prominent Democrats who stayed in the national Democratic Party throughout their political careers? Why doesn't that make the Democratic Party the party of racism?

Literally hundreds and hundreds of segregationists and racist Democratic officeholders across the South, including U.S.

senators, members of the House of Representatives, and prominent governors, remained loyal to the Democratic Party until the end of their days and remained welcome in the Democratic Party.

These progressive Democrats were also backers of Franklin D. Roosevelt, one of the most liberal presidents in the history of the United States. The U.S. Senate especially was a hotbed of southern Democrat racists, including Robert Byrd (of KKK fame), Allen Ellender, Sam Ervin, Albert Gore, Sr., James Eastland, J. William Fulbright, Walter F. George, Ernest Hollings, Russell Long, Richard Russell, John Stennis, and Herman Talmadge, to name just a few.

But it wasn't just liberal racist Senators who stayed in the Democratic Party. It was also racist Democrat governors such as Ross Barnett, John Bell Williams, George Wallace (who later bolted to run as an independent for president), Fob James, Earl Long, Jimmie Davis, Jimmy Byrnes, and Orval Faubus, who remained in the Democratic Party to the day of their death. The governors in particular were instrumental in blocking school integration. Arkansas Governor Orval Faubus, in defiance of the 1954 Supreme Court ruling, infamously refused to protect nine black students who sought to attend Little Rock's all-white Central High School.[306] And let's not forget the notorious Sheriff Bull Connor, who used fire hoses and dogs to break up peaceful civil rights demonstrations in the South. Connor remained a Democrat till the day he died.[307]

What about so-called New Democrats from the South such as Bill Clinton? Did Clinton ever publicly condemn Senator William Fulbright for voting against every civil rights act? Did liberal northern Democrats or liberal publications shun Fulbright? No; they didn't kick him out of the Democratic Party even when he signed the Southern Manifesto opposing the U.S. Supreme Court's *Brown v. Board of Education* ruling that ended the segregation of public schools.[308] Nothing could diminish the love that liberals had for William Fulbright. In fact, just three years after

Fulbright voted against the 1965 Voting Rights Act, Bill Clinton worked on his reelection campaign. And lest there be any doubt about Clinton's deep affection and respect for Senator Fulbright, President Clinton gave the old segregationist the Presidential Medal of Freedom in 1993.[309] Was Clinton accused of being a racist for doing that? No, of course not. And when President Clinton said of Fulbright, *"If it hadn't been for him I don't think I'd be here today,"*[310] was there a protest? Not at all. Yet when Donald Trump posthumously bestowed the Presidential Medal of Freedom on Elvis Presley, Chris Richards, the music critic of the *Washington Post,* criticized the president, accusing him of *"sending a message"* to the racists of America that *"black visionaries could invent rock-and-roll, but only a white man could become king."* Richards went on to describe giving the award to Presley as *"ugly."*[311] As the saying goes, if it weren't for double standards, liberals would have no standards at all.

Yet even today William Fulbright is hailed as a champion of liberal causes. However, in its obituary of Fulbright, even the *Washington Post* had to admit, *"His record in the Senate on civil rights was something else again: it was dismal. He not only voted against all the laws which in the fifties and sixties transformed this nation, he filibustered against them in company with some of the worst racists ever to serve in the Senate."*[312]

Fulbright wasn't just in the company of some of the worst racists in the Senate, he was one of them, as his actions proved. The bottom line is that by overwhelming numbers, racist progressive Democrats and their segregationist followers stayed in the Democratic Party.

Fortunately, the period after World War II brought many changes to the South. For instance, air-conditioning made manufacturing possible there. Large corporations found business-friendly tax policies in the South and moved there. That in turn brought millions of midwesterners and northeasterners to the South. *"These 'immigrants' identified themselves as Republicans at higher rates than native whites,"*[313] and they rejected the racism of the entrenched Democratic Party. Meanwhile, the number of southern children attending college, black and white, was growing. Whereas the racists overwhelmingly remained in the Democratic Party, enlightened and educated whites who supported free enterprise and not the big-government policies of the Democrats drifted toward the Republican Party. These new Republicans were embarrassed by and unsupportive of the racist policies of the Democratic Party and its friends in the Ku Klux Klan. Christian evangelicals in the South,[314] many of whom supported the civil rights movement of the 1960s, were no longer comfortable with a Democratic Party that supported abortion and Planned Parenthood. These New South Republicans rejected segregation, racism, and bigotry and were fearful of the cradle-to-grave government promoted by the Democratic Party: *"The evidence suggests that the GOP advanced in the South because it attracted much the same upwardly mobile (and non-union) economic and religious conservatives that it did elsewhere in the country."*[315]

In short, these New South Republicans embraced a better future for the people of their region, both black and white. Many of the liberal Democrats, in contrast, not only clung to their racist past but were soft on communism and favored high taxes, big government, and expanded social welfare programs. This created a special opportunity for Republicans in the South. One of the new successful Republicans was Winthrop Rockefeller, a pro-integration moderate conservative who succeeded rabid Democrat segregationist Orval Faubus as governor of Arkansas in 1966.[316] In 1966, another conservative Republican was elected in the South, Howard Baker, who also ran on an integrationist platform.[317] Later, Baker would serve as President Ronald Reagan's chief of staff.

It is important to note that not all the old-line progressive southern Democrats continued in their misguided embrace of segregation and white superiority; many, if not most, eventually rejected their racist past, as did Senator Strom Thurmond. And it would be unfair to imply that ardent liberals such as Senator Hubert Humphrey of Minnesota did not support civil rights for black Americans; he did. Nevertheless, liberals like Humphrey were often a minority in the Democratic Party when it came to civil rights.

But, liberals will protest: What about the Southern Strategy of Richard Nixon in 1968? Wasn't it an overt racist appeal to redneck racists in the South? It was not, and neither was the appeal by Barry Goldwater, as we now know. It was simply a recognition that the South had rejected its progressive past in favor of a more conservative approach to government. A study conducted by the Claremont Institute compared the appeal of Goldwater in the South with his appeal nationwide.[318] In both speeches and written documents, the appeal was identical. It was an appeal based on constitutional government, anticommunism, free enterprise, and low taxes. Yet numerous scholars and writers continue to argue that in 1964 Goldwater used "coded" language[319] to appeal to segregationists in the South.

This is not only a dishonest smear, it is irrational because it ignores facts and logic. If indeed Barry Goldwater intentionally appealed to white segregationists in the South, it follows logically that he would have touted his vote against the Civil Rights Act of 1964 in his speeches and stated or at least implied that he would not enforce the 1964 Civil Rights law in the South. After all, if Goldwater was soliciting the votes of segregationists, he would of necessity have to make it clear that he was of one mind with them. Did he do that?

To the contrary, even in the final week of his 1964 presidential campaign, Goldwater went into the heart of the Deep South, Columbia, South Carolina, and condemned segregation, declaring *"all men as equal in the arena of law and civil order."*[320] Then Goldwater went on to pledge that if he was elected president, he would implement and enforce all the provisions of the

Civil Rights Act of 1964. Goldwater didn't say this just in South Carolina; this pro–civil rights speech was televised on 87 stations across the South.[321] Goldwater was indeed sending a message; it was a clear, bold declaration that as president he would fully enforce the 1964 Civil Rights Act and advance the cause of civil rights while in office. So much for Goldwater sending messages, coded or uncoded, to southern racists and segregationists that he stood with them! Goldwater made it clear that he had no interest whatsoever in tolerating discrimination against black Americans anywhere in the nation.

Ironically, considering the hardened racism of Lyndon Johnson *after* he signed the 1964 Civil Rights Bill, it is not only possible but also very likely that the enforcement of the Civil Rights Act of 1964 by a President Barry Goldwater would have been more determined and effective than was that by Lyndon Johnson. In fact, the record shows that Johnson made no effort at all to end segregation in the South. Instead, it was left to Richard Nixon of the so-called Southern Strategy to do that, and as we now know, he did.[322]

Today's South is a region bustling with economic growth and prosperity beyond that which existed during any time in American history. That prosperity came about thanks to Republican governors, Republican senators and congressmen, and Republican majorities in state legislatures across the South. It was Republicans who believed in low taxes, limited regulations, and small government who created a new, prosperous South, certainly not the high-tax, big-government liberal Democrats.

As a result of the changes in the South, the original great migration of black Americans from the South to the North came to an end in 1970, and that year a new black American migration from the North to the South began. This remigration of black Americans to the South included not only young black professionals but also retirees who were welcomed into small towns and big cities alike. Between 2005 and 2010, two-thirds of all moves by black Americans were to the South, not from it. This remigration *"also testifies to the liberal North's failure to integrate African-Americans into the mainstream."*[323]

More important, this remigration is a testimony to the dramatic change in attitude by white Americans in the South toward black Americans. How significant is this remigration? According to William Frey, a Brookings Institution demographer, the remigration of black Americans to the South that *"began as a trickle in the 1970s, increased in the 1990s, and turned into a virtual evacuation from many northern areas in the first decade of the 2000s."*[324]

One of those young black professionals who migrated to the South was Angelo Byrd,[325] who moved from Toledo, Ohio, to Atlanta, Georgia. After living his entire life in Toledo, Angelo happened upon an opportunity to move to Atlanta at age 25. The move from Ohio has turned out well. Byrd became director of transportation for J.B. Hunt, a very large transportation company. *"I feel more comfortable in a place where black people are doing important things. I feel there is more of an advantage to being here,"*[326] Angelo said.

Others are like Darlene Cox, who was born and raised in Chicago but moved to a tiny town in Mississippi.[327] When her husband first suggested moving to Mississippi upon his retirement from General Motors, Darlene was resistant. Although she had never lived in the South, as a young girl she had traveled to Tunica, Mississippi, where she had relatives. She loved her relatives but was not fond of the racist and dangerous Mississippi she knew as a child. Nevertheless, her husband, Charlie, persuaded her to make the move. When Darlene was interviewed by the *Christian Science Monitor* in 2014, she was enthusiastic about her move to a small town in the South, saying, *"I wouldn't [trade] anything for West Point now. It's quiet here."* Her husband agreed.[328] Angelo Byrd, Darlene Cox, and her husband, Charlie, are the kinds of black Americans who are probably supportive of the record level of prosperity created by the policies of Donald Trump.

Thanks to the mild weather and a newfound racial harmony, black and white Americans continue to move southward to places where Americans of all races prosper, socialize, and work together. This fact belies the false narrative that Republicans came to power in the South through appeals to racism. In fact, today's South not only includes the first popularly elected black Republican U.S. Senator, Tim Scott, of South Carolina but also the first elected black Republican congressman from Texas, Will Hurd. As black Americans in the South reevaluate the Republican Party and increasingly see it as the party of jobs, opportunity, quality education for their children, and traditional moral values, the success of the GOP in the South is likely to continue.

The simple truth is that thanks to Donald Trump, the Democrats' baseless cries of racism are losing credibility with black Americans, especially young black Americans. The more strident and outrageous the smears become, such as Vice President Biden saying in a speech to black Americans about Republicans, *"They're going to put you all back in chains"*[329] and *"Trump, Republicans [are] allowing Jim Crow to return,"*[330] the less believable the smears become. Democrats tell black Americans not to believe their eyes when it comes to the policies of Donald Trump creating the lowest black unemployment and highest wages in recorded American history.[331] Perhaps that is why President Trump's approval rating among black Americans reached 40 percent in the fall of 2018.[332]

Thanks in part to Donald Trump directly appealing to black voters and addressing their most pressing problems, the nasty false narrative made up by the Democrats that all Republicans are racists is dying.

CHAPTER 11

Abandonment

Although Donald Trump often speaks out about the tragedy of young black men being slaughtered by the thousands in big Democratic-controlled cities across the nation, liberals remain silent. They completely ignore the deaths of those poor black Americans. Democrats know as well as Republicans that the overwhelming majority of those who live in communities plagued by violence are law-abiding citizens. In fact, *"most from these communities also hold the law in high esteem, and believe there should be consequences for not following it."*[333] Yet these good people live in fear of the violent gangs that wreak havoc in their communities. They are threatened daily with violence and harm, and too often an innocent child or adult is killed by a random bullet in a shoot-out between gangs. In Chicago, thousands of young men in gangs, as well as innocent bystanders, have been killed over the last few years.[334]

When it is bitter cold outside, the shootings decline, but when good weather comes along, they resume immediately. For example, during one 24-hour period in April 2019, when the weather warmed up, *"24 people were shot in Chicago, including three children under 13."*[335] In 2018, there were a total of 2,948 shooting victims in Chicago.[336] Thanks to the valiant efforts of the Chicago police, that number was down significantly from 3,463 victims in 2017 and 4,351 in 2016.[337] Nevertheless, nearly 3,000 shootings is a dreadful number, and living in a community where most of those shootings take place is understandably terrifying.

But has any major Democrat politician spoken out publicly about the shootings and presented a plan to make those neighborhoods safe again? No, there hasn't been one. Like Hillary Clinton, who called young black men with guns *"super predators,"*[338] liberal Democrats don't offer any solution to this terrible problem. Yet they have the audacity to keep asking for the votes of black Americans. They expect to receive monolithic black support in spite of the fact that it was liberal policies dating back to Lyndon Johnson's War on Poverty that ultimately resulted in breaking up the black family. Fathers were driven out of black homes, resulting in fatherless young black men turning to gangs and violence to prove their manhood. Consider just how far down this road America has gone: *"Prior to the mid-1960s, nearly all children were born to married couples. When the War on Poverty began in 1964, only 7 percent of children were born to unmarried women."*[339] However, by 2017, 69.4 percent of all black births occurred outside of marriage.[340]

Daniel Patrick Moynihan, who served as assistant secretary of labor in the Johnson administration, issued a warning about an impending breakdown of the black family as a result of the absence of fathers in black families: *"In his 1965 'The Negro Family: The Case for National Action,' Moynihan observed that because more blacks were being born into unmarried homes, more blacks were becoming dependent on welfare to survive."*[341]

Moynihan's warning was ridiculed, and he was accused of *"subtle racism."*[342] As a result of the destruction of intact homes with mothers and fathers, the problem of violence in black communities increased dramatically. By ridiculing Moynihan's warning and denying young black boys a father to serve as a role model, liberals fostered the gang violence that exists in America's big cities today. They further ensured that result by denying high-quality schools to black Americans. This is a betrayal and an abandonment of black Americans by the left. Today's radical Democrats are driven by an ideology that looks down on marriage and blames people like Moynihan for racism rather than dealing with the disaster their welfare policy has brought to black Americans.

There is another reason liberal/progressive Democrats are abandoning black Americans. It's a political reason, and it has to do with simple numbers. As the number of Hispanics (both legal and illegal) expands in the United States, their votes become much more important to the Democrats than the votes of black Americans. Although 13.4 percent of the total U.S. population consists of black people, the Hispanic population now accounts for 18.1 percent of the U.S. population.[343] One hundred thousand illegals came into the United States across our southern border in 2018,[344] and more than a million illegals will cross over into our nation in 2019.[345] The Democrats see nothing wrong with this. The Democrats' plan is simple. Once they regain total power—Congress and the White House—they will grant amnesty to most illegal aliens, giving them the vote. That's why liberal Democrats such as Robert Francis "Beto" O'Rourke want to tear down the border wall and let millions of Hispanics, including dangerous MS-13 members, come into the United States.[346] It comes down to simple math. Why should the Democrats care about black voters when they can have the votes of millions of poor Hispanic voters, many of whom will take jobs away from poor black Americans? Democratic partisans may scoff, but *"Vernon Briggs, Emeritus Professor of Labor Economics at Cornell University, testified before the U.S. Commission on Civil Rights that there was 'little doubt' that black Americans are the 'major loser' in the immigration equation."*[347]

Think about the Democrats' record. Politics and power have always come before the well-being of black Americans. It doesn't make any difference what the issue is. Schools? They choose the money from the teachers union over poor black children getting a good education. Planned Parenthood? They choose the money from Planned Parenthood over the lives of unborn black children. Green New Deal? Democrats always choose higher gasoline, electric, and fuel prices, disregarding the burden it places on poor black families. Manufacturing jobs that pay well? Obama ridiculed Donald Trump for suggesting that he would bring back manufacturing jobs, condescendingly asking him if he had a *"magic wand."*[348] Socialism? The Democrats would willingly eliminate the opportunity for black Americans to climb the economic ladder in order to impose a Venezuelan or Cuban type of socialism on all Americans.

To progressive Democrats, the poor—black, white, Asian, Hispanic—are always expendable in their quest for a utopia. Their obsession with the unproven theory of human-caused global warming always takes precedence over the needs of the poor, not only in our nation but especially in South America as well as in Africa. The reality is that if the radical environmental agenda of the left is fully implemented, the nations of Africa will be destined never to emerge from poverty. The 2018–2019 riots in France provide evidence of the reaction of poor families to the artificial increase of fuel oil, gasoline, and diesel prices caused by adherence to the Paris Agreement.[349] The exact same thing would have taken place here in the United States if Hillary Clinton had been elected president and insisted that the United States honor and participate in the Paris accords. And it will happen here if the Democrats regain control of the White House and Congress in 2020.

This is both sad and foolish, especially in light of the fact that a recent United Nations report stated that more than 2 billion people have been lifted out of extreme poverty over the last 25 years thanks to technology, the spread of economic freedom, and the expansion of trade.[350] But instead of economic freedom, progressive Democrats push for a more controlled, top-down socialist economy in which decisions about where you live, how much water you can use, how much electricity you use, what kind of car you drive, what you eat, and how you heat and cool your home and when you can do it are to be decided by government bureaucrats.

Most recently, radical socialist leaders such as Alexandria Ocasio-Cortez have called for an end to air travel in ten years, the elimination of cows, the reconstruction of every building in the United States, and a total ban on the use of oil and gas for heating.[351] In addition, leading Democrats are promising free cradle-to-grave education, jobs for everyone who wants to work, and pay for those who don't.[352] It is pure pie-in-the-sky utopian nonsense, but already more than 100 Democratic members of Congress have endorsed the catastrophic Green New Deal plan.[353] The entire radical environmental agenda is just a means of gaining more power and control over the life of every American. This goal once again makes the poor expendable in the eyes of Democrats, just as they considered black Americans expendable under slavery and then under segregation.

Perhaps it is this attitude by liberal Democrats, combined with the open arms of President Trump, that has encouraged black Americans to take a second look at the Republican Party. Citing his high polling support among black Americans, the president said at an Oval Office meeting with black leaders, *"The Democrats are very nervous. They do nothing for you."*[354] The president was, of course, right. One of those who took a second look at conservatism and the Republican Party was Vernon Robinson.

CHAPTER 12

Left-to-Right Odyssey

My deceased father, Vernon Robinson, Jr., was a Tuskegee Airman who fixed radios on the P-51 Mustang in Italy during World War II. After being released from duty with the Army Air Corps, my father was employed by the Civil Aeronautics Aviation Administration (now the FAA). After several stops in other places, including Hawaii, he ended up in Los Angeles, eventually becoming a supervisor.

That's where my siblings and I grew up, and that's where I began to understand discrimination against black Americans. At one point, my mother told me that first Crenshaw Boulevard and then La Brea Avenue was a dividing line between black and white home owners. If you were black, you couldn't buy a house on the western side of that line. Our family lived in the Watts area, which was then a lower-middle-class neighborhood, not the dangerous place it is today. In fact, when I was a kindergartner, my brother, my sister, and I walked six blocks to school without my mother worrying about our safety. But by the time I was an adult, my mother would discourage me from walking those six blocks in daylight, let alone at night.

Growing up, my siblings and I heard many stories of discrimination from my mother. As was related earlier in this book, she was a civil rights pioneer from early in her life. You already know about her efforts in 1944 as a nursing student in New Orleans to register to vote and how she was threatened with lynching. But that didn't stop her; instead, I believe it made her more determined. My mother was well educated and smart. In fact, she was the first black faculty member in a four-year baccalaureate degree nursing program in California. Once a pioneer, always a pioneer.

Although I was aware of discrimination in Los Angeles, it wasn't until I was ten that I first saw Jim Crow[355] segregation in the South up close and personal. In 1965, we piled into our station wagon and drove from Los Angeles to Franklin, Louisiana, where my mother's family lived. Thinking back now, I realize that it was only because of the passage of the 1964 Civil Rights Act that my family could stay at Travelodges and Holiday Inns in Texas and elsewhere in the South. If the trip had happened three years earlier, before passage of the Civil Rights Act of 1964 that guaranteed black Americans equal access to public accommodations, we probably wouldn't have been able to stay in those motels. Instead, our family would have been forced to stay in less than ideal black boardinghouses, if we could find them.

I found out quickly that although there was discrimination in California, it was not as open and ugly as it was in the South in 1965. Even as a 10-year-old child, I was stunned when I saw three bathrooms at gas stations and other public facilities labeled Men, Women, and Colored. That was when I began to appreciate a little bit of what my mother and her family in Louisiana were forced to put up with. It wasn't just the attitude that black people were inferior to white people that was so repugnant; it was also the unfair way black men and women and especially black children were treated. Despite the discrimination that existed in Los Angeles, my two sisters and I came back to California with a new appreciation of how fortunate we were to not live in the South.

My mother, of course, who grew up in the South of the 1930s and 1940s, experienced the inhuman degradation of segregation. Despite having a brilliant mind, my mother received a poor public education from the segregated school she was forced to attend. In the South of my mother's day, only a small fraction of the money that was spent per white student was spent to educate black students.[356] It seems that separate wasn't equal.

After high school, my mother enrolled at Dillard University in New Orleans. But sadly, there was a problem. The college president could tell that although my mother was smart, she had not received a good enough education to succeed at Dillard. He bluntly but honestly told her that she was not ready for college-level work. Instead, he arranged for her to catch up by attending Gilbert Academy, which, frankly, she really wasn't ready for either.

My very determined mother was not deterred. She worked extremely hard to catch up, but then she ran into another roadblock to getting a college education. She had only enough money to attend Gilbert Academy for one semester. When the dorm matron asked her why she was leaving, she said, *"Well, ma'am, I'm not coming back. I only had enough money for one semester, so I'm going home. I hope you have a Merry Christmas. I won't be seeing you again."*[357]

The dorm matron was so distressed by my mother's situation that she talked to the headmistress of Gilbert Academy about the matter. The headmistress didn't want to lose a smart, hardworking student like my mother, and so she offered her a way to stay in school. She said that if my mother would clean her house and work in the cafeteria, she would pay her tuition. Of course, my mother was overjoyed. That act of kindness and generosity enabled my mother to remain at Gilbert Academy, and after she successfully completed her studies there, some anonymous person generously paid her tuition at Dillard. To this day, my mother doesn't know who the anonymous person was, but she remains thankful for that person's great kindness. I don't know how much the anonymous donor contributed to make my mother's college education possible, but whoever it was got a fantastic return on his or her investment. I am proud to say that my mother graduated as the number two nursing student at the school, second only to her roommate, who was number one.

A sort of sad but humorous episode took place when my mother first arrived at Gilbert Academy. As was done with all new students at that time, my mother was taken on a tour of the school library. My mother was astounded that she could check out and read any of the books. She just couldn't believe it, because the public library in Franklin where she grew up did not allow any black person to check out a book. In fact, my mother was so excited that while a student at Gilbert Academy, she checked out and read as many books as possible for fear that the library might change the rules to be the same as the public library in Franklin. As we grew older, my siblings and I kidded her, saying that she must have learned a lot. She laughs about it, but the idea that a black person could not make use of the public library is shocking and just plain cruel.

My brother, my sister, and I were considered star students at our local public school in Los Angeles, but my mother was determined that we would have the best free education we could get. One summer, my mother drove the three of us 25 miles each way to the University Elementary School, a lab school on the campus of UCLA. It was a summer program mostly for the children of the faculty. We were entitled to attend, but only during the summer. My sister, my brother, and I thought attending the lab school all summer was the best thing since sliced bread. We, as well as our mother, were elated when we finally were allowed to attend the lab school full time three years later. Conversely, the teachers at the local school were very unhappy, because this meant they would be losing three very good and generally well behaved students. I was fortunate to spend my last year and a half of elementary school at the lab school.

The first time I was called N-word to my face was when I was 13, and to this day I clearly remember the bitter taste of adrenaline in my mouth when it happened. Ironically, it didn't happen in California or even in the South. In fact, I was the one black kid in the group going to the Japanese Boy Scout jamboree in Asagiri Heights, Japan, at the foot of Mount Fuji. A fellow Asian American in our group uttered that awful word.

But the truth is, I didn't have it nearly as hard as my parents, especially my mother, who grew up in rural Louisiana. Even the Catholic Church was racist in Franklin, Louisiana, in the late 1930s. After attending a Catholic Church and taking instruction classes as a child, my mother was supposed to participate in her first communion. She was dressed in white like the other girls and was ready to march into the church during the ceremony, when she was told that because she was black, she couldn't participate with the rest of the girls. I can only imagine how it must have hurt my mother. Understandably, from that point forward, my mother was finished with the Catholic Church.

As you can imagine, my parents weren't Republicans, although I found out recently that my father was a registered Republican in the 1940s and later switched to the Democrats. Naturally, when the Republican nominee for president, Barry Goldwater, voted against the 1964 Civil Rights Act, that was the last straw for my parents and for millions of black Americans. The Civil Rights Act of 1964, which gave great protection to black Americans in exercising their rights, was truly a godsend. If you aren't black, you can't possibly imagine what it was like to finally have full rights as an American citizen. Having the right to stay where you want to stay and eat where you want to eat was so incredible. White Americans took that simple right for granted, but for black Americans this new freedom was exhilarating. For the first time, really, it was as if you were truly an American citizen equal under the law to everyone else. It wasn't that there was racial harmony, but passage of the Civil Rights Act of 1964 was a huge, historic step for black Americans. However untrue, I still remember the assessment of the 1964 election from adults in the alley behind my house. A neighbor said, "Goldwater, dirty water, the Republicans ain't done nuthin' for us."

In truth, there was very little racial harmony in the 1960s, but in my view, it improved gradually until just after the turn of the twenty-first century. Unfortunately, America backslid then largely because Democrats in general and the Obama administration in particular used racial division for political gain. They intentionally encouraged racial division to ensure that they would retain the black vote on Election Day. That set racial harmony and comity between the races back significantly. Instead of a postracial society as some hoped for with the election of Barack Obama, the racial divide increased.

Originally, I believed that the concept of affirmative action was sound. It caused companies to recruit black students first on northern campuses and later on all campuses across the nation. That was a good outcome. But eventually affirmative action programs worsened racial relations. Understandably, white Americans became suspicious that the black Americans who worked beside them got into college because of affirmative action, not because they were equally talented and educated. Similarly, when a black person was promoted, there was suspicion that he was promoted because he was black, not because he was the most qualified person. Even today, the idea lingers that if you are black and successful, you somehow got there because of affirmative action, not because of your actual talents, hard work, and merit. This suspicion strains racial relations.

If you maintain the same standards for black and white students, affirmative action works, but if you put your thumb on the scale and accept a less qualified black student just because he is black, it defeats the purpose of affirmative action and exacerbates race relations. There's no doubt that it was wrong to exclude black students from colleges across the nation, but admitting someone to college who is less qualified to compete against more qualified students nearly guarantees failure for that student. Sadly, racism is alive and well, especially on the left, and it is often made worse by well-meaning yet poorly thought out public policy.

How did I come to this conclusion? How did I become a conservative? When I went to high school, I joined a socialist group. Our main endeavor was to publish a left-wing underground newspaper called the *Red Tide*. I suspect that we did not make any converts, and I wasn't what you might call an informed socialist. As crazy as it sounds, the real reason I joined the socialists was that I was afraid of girls when I was in high school. I didn't have the courage even to ask a girl to have a hamburger and Coke with me. Instead, I tried to be cool by adopting a radical persona, wearing an army jacket and a big Afro. It was easy to be a socialist since as a high school student I didn't have to actually put food on the table; I had the luxury to fantasize about how great socialism would be.

The truth is, I was still a leftist when I first attended the Air Force Academy. But during my four years at the academy, my views began to change. It was clear to me that the Democratic Party was weak on foreign and defense policy. I knew that such weakness would get Americans killed. In my sophomore year at the academy, North Korea seized the U.S. Navy ship *Pueblo*. I was shocked. How could a fourth-rate power seize an American vessel? When I graduated in 1977, I was no longer a socialist, but I was still comfortable with the liberal policies of the Democratic Party.

When the Soviet Union invaded Afghanistan in 1979 and President Jimmy Carter seemed shocked, again I didn't understand it. How could the president be shocked if he was a Naval Academy graduate? Didn't President Carter understand the aggressive nature of the Soviet Union? Didn't he understand that they intended to conquer the world?

Eventually, I concluded that the Democrats not only had a weak foreign and defense policy but also had bought into cultural decay, especially their love affair with abortion on demand and then their acceptance of homosexual marriage. I was certainly moving to the right, although I might not have been consciously aware of it.

Undoubtedly, the most important factor in my conversion to conservatism was Milton Friedman's book *Free to Choose*. The fellow who gave me Friedman's book was an accounting professor. He said, "Vernon, you need to read this book." That's what I did, and for the first time I gained a practical understanding of economic reality. I began to understand why freedom and free markets always work and why socialism always fails.

However, as an Air Force officer on active duty, I was not allowed to be involved with partisan politics. Nevertheless, I concluded that the country was going to hell and knew I had to do my best to save it. But what should I do? I felt that the American political system was corrupt and dirty. Fortuitously, at that time, I was doing some graduate work in international affairs and my professor allowed me to do an independent study of constitutional law, which I loved. He also arranged for me to receive three semester hours of credit as an intern for a state representative in Kansas City, not far from Warrensburg, where I was stationed. I was dubious about being involved in politics, but to my surprise I got hooked. This is how it happened.

The state representative, Alan Wheat, was a 27-year-old black Democrat who was a rising political star. Alan was a sharp and effective politician who knew how to play the game. Clearly, I didn't understand it at all. It was all new to me. For example, once Alan took me to meet union leaders at a working-class bar. Union leaders were important players in the Democratic Party. They asked me what I wanted to drink. I said, "I'll have an Amaretto," and I saw Alan roll his eyes. After the union guys left, Alan said, "Is there anybody else drinking an Italian liquor here?" His point was that politics is about fitting in. If everybody was drinking a beer, you drank a beer. My political education was beginning.

One evening Alan took me to a meeting with the Democratic speaker of the Missouri House of Representatives at a bar across from the Federal Building in Kansas City. The topic of the Equal Rights Amendment came up. The speaker said that it was not going to pass in the Missouri House, because he knew that if he forced a party line vote, many of his Democratic members in rural areas would lose in the next election. Considering that political reality, he told Alan that he was going to release the Democrat members to vote in accordance with the views of the majority of voters in their individual districts. Practical politics caused the ERA to go down to defeat in the Missouri legislature. As a newcomer, I was stunned because I had just seen the Equal Rights Amendment go down to defeat over drinks at a bar. At that moment, the internship that I thought would get me out of politics instead pulled me into politics.

State Representative Wheat decided to run for the U.S. Congress the year I was leaving the Air Force, and he offered me a job on his campaign staff. He laughed when I told him that I had decided to leave the area and go back to California to work in a Republican campaign.

How did I decide I wanted to be a Republican? My journey to the GOP began with a black woman who was a Republican county supervisor in Kansas City, Joanne Collins. I had moved to the right intellectually, but I wasn't quite certain I was ready to join the Republican Party. A black person being a Republican officeholder was practically unheard of in 1981, so I thought she could help me out. I met with her, and she said, "You look like a pretty smart young man. You can do well in the Republican Party." She made the Republican Party sound like the party of opportunity for a young smart black man, so I took her advice and became a Republican.

Something else factored into my decision to join the Republican Party. I asked myself what the three most important problems facing the black community were. I concluded that those problems were

- The destruction of the black family by the welfare state

- The collapse of quality public education as a means of upward mobility for black Americans
- The lack of entrepreneurial business activity by black Americans

In looking at each of those issues, I concluded that the Democratic Party wasn't addressing any of them. Democrats controlled both sides of the dependency lobby: the people who ran the Department of Social Services and the welfare recipients. I could see that there was no way the Democratic Party would ever reform welfare.

I was very proud of myself having figured that out in 1981, considering that it took the Republican revolution of 1994 for those issues to be addressed. I was very pleased when House Speaker Newt Gingrich and the Republican majority passed welfare reform. Regarding education, I realized that the teachers union was a very powerful constituency of the Democratic Party and that that meant the Democrats would never support school vouchers, which I believe to be the key to quality education for poor black children. My conclusion was that the Democrats would never agree to the reforms that were needed to make it possible for black Americans to succeed economically. Finally, I concluded that the Republican Party offered the only real hope for black Americans to restore quality education, the only ladder out of poverty for the poor.

I heard Republicans talk about the importance of increasing entrepreneurial activity in black communities, but the Democrats said nothing about that. Democrats say they love employees, but they hate employers and wage a class war of envy against the clever productive people who create jobs for the rest of us. How could the Democrats be champions of entrepreneurial activity in the black community?

Considering the cultural shift, the Democrats' weakness in foreign and defense policy, their affinity for the welfare state, their unwillingness to buck the teachers union, their opposition to choice schools, and their lack of interest in entrepreneurism, I was left with no choice but to become a Republican.

My first successful foray into politics was a campaign for the Winston-Salem City Council, to which I was elected in 1997 and reelected in 2001. One day as a councilman I received an e-mail from a young black lady that was quite humorous. She said, "I need to ask you something, councilman. Why are you Republican? I'm not trying to be funny. I don't know any Republicans. My family doesn't know any Republicans. My husband's family doesn't know any Republicans."

I responded to her e-mail by explaining why I became a Republican and how Democrats finance groups like Planned Parenthood that target black babies for abortion. I explained how the Democrats had abandoned traditional values and said that in my opinion Republicans were the only hope for black Americans. After she received my e-mail, she responded, saying, "My husband just came back and said that if the Democratic Party is for killing babies and supports homosexual marriage, we can't be for that. We are going to register as Republicans."

And they did.

It's my belief that many other black Americans are coming to the same conclusion that I came to years ago and that this couple came to. Today's Democratic Party not only takes black votes for granted, it no longer cares about the welfare and success of black people. In fact, it fears that if black Americans become prosperous and successful, they will no longer vote Democratic. There's just no indication that they are willing to implement reforms in education such as school choice, quit targeting black babies for abortion, institute programs to restore the black family, or encourage policies that will give black Americans upward economic mobility. And with many black Americans, the Democratic strategy to paint all Republicans as racist is losing credibility. As black Americans see the very real improvement in their economic situation under Donald Trump and as he makes a straightforward, candid appeal to them, more of them will think seriously about voting for Donald Trump in 2020. I may have been one of the early converts to conservatism and the GOP, but there are plenty of others who are now coming back to the party of Abraham Lincoln and Donald Trump.

CHAPTER 13

Disillusioned

An increasing number of black Americans are becoming disillusioned with today's far-left Democratic Party. But will they vote for Donald Trump in 2020? Black American hesitancy to vote for a Republican candidate for president is understandable but also regrettable when you consider the low regard in which black Americans are held by today's progressive Democrats. All that radical Democrats seem to care about is black votes, not black success and black prosperity. And truthfully, the Republicans haven't always been much better. That's why black Americans stayed in the Democratic Party until Donald Trump came along.

Make no mistake about it: Today's Democratic Party is no longer the Democratic Party of John F. Kennedy. If it was, Donald Trump probably would still be a Democrat as he was most of his life. Sadly, that pro-life, pro-God, low-tax, pro-jobs, pro–civil rights, pro-America party is long gone. It's been taken over by left-wing radicals who want to flood our nation with illegals who take away jobs that otherwise would go to black Americans and other minorities.[358] These new Democrats ardently support abortion mills run by Planned Parenthood that target black babies for destruction.[359] And Democrats couldn't care less if they double or triple the price of heating fuel and gasoline, a move that economically cripples poor black families and makes it all the more difficult to escape from poverty.[360]

Tragically, these new Democrats want nothing whatsoever to do with the God that millions of Americans, black, white, Asian, and Hispanic, worship in church each Sunday. Echoing the leaders of the French Revolution, these new radical Democrats have decided that God really doesn't exist, or if he does, they no longer want or need him.[361] For political expediency, Democrats choose the teachers union over the welfare of young black students when they fight against placing high-quality choice schools in poor black areas.[362] Hypocritically, Democrats send their own children to private schools[363] but gladly let poor black children attend inferior schools that destine them to failure in life. Democrats in big cities pass regulations and require spurious certifications that effectively bar black men and women from competing with government-sanctioned monopolies such as taxi service, barbershops, and beauty salons.

Today's radical Democrats endanger all Americans but especially poor Americans. By opposing construction of a wall on our southern border to keep out drugs, drug dealers, illegal guns, MS-13 gang members, sex traffickers, and tens of thousands of unskilled illegal immigrants, they make it harder for poor black Americans to climb the economic ladder of success. The only logical conclusion is that the Democrats are more concerned about the welfare of illegal aliens than about the welfare of black Americans.

Unlike President John F. Kennedy, this new breed of Democrats unanimously opposes tax cuts[364] and other commonsense economic measures that have been advanced by President Trump. It is these policies which have created the lowest black unemployment in American history and the highest wages for black Americans in decades.[365] Unfortunately, the wage gap between black and white workers remains high and will be eliminated only when Democrats quit blocking choice schools for poor black children, allowing them to get the high-quality education that is necessary for success.

Although the previous Democratic administration repeatedly promised much-needed prison reform, President Donald Trump made it happen.[366] Today, thousands of nonviolent black inmates not only are being set free but also are receiving job training so that they can become productive members of society. For Donald Trump this is not about politics; it's about doing what is right.

In stark contrast, winning the next election is more important to Democrats than taking care of the real problems facing America's black community or bringing harmony and reconciliation to our land. In fact, the last thing cynical Democrats want is racial harmony and reconciliation. These new Democrats, who even booed God at their national convention,[367] have absolutely no interest in preserving America's wonderful legacy of Christian charity and forgiveness. Where there is no forgiveness, there can be no unity.

Of course, America is not a Christian country by law, but it is by consensus, and black Americans are among the most Christian[368] and charitable[369] individuals in our nation. In fact, it is our common values derived from the Bible that have helped bind us together and are the reason America has overcome and will continue to overcome such terrible problems as slavery, segregation, and the racial disharmony we still face today. After all, it was black Christians led by a black Christian pastor, Dr. Martin Luther King, Jr., who deserve full credit for the success of the 1950s and 1960s civil rights movement. The courage, fortitude, and perseverance of Dr. King changed America forever and for good.

But why are black Americans turning to Donald Trump? The answer is that Trump has proved that he can be trusted. One by one he has fulfilled his campaign promises. But from the day he came down the escalator at Trump Tower to announce his candidacy for president, the entrenched political establishment hated and derided Donald Trump because he promised to drain the swamp—their swamp—and they didn't like that. Establishment Republicans and establishment Democrats alike hated the very thought of an outsider like Donald Trump becoming president and upsetting their self-serving way of doing business. This attitude is epitomized by the seemingly unhinged attack on President Trump by former CIA director John Brennan, who said, "*When the full extent of your venality, moral turpitude, and political corruption becomes known, you will take your rightful place as a disgraced demagogue in the dustbin of history. . . . America will triumph over you.*"[370] Brennan, of course, equates America with the Washington, D.C., establishment, that is, the swamp. His unhinged tone probably is caused by the knowledge that he has committed illegal acts to take down a sitting president and that prosecution of those felonies could put him behind bars. Brennan and other deep state actors seek to run government to serve themselves and their globalist objectives. Establishment Republicans and Democrats have fought Donald Trump every step of the way, but the people spoke.

On November 8, 2016, old-line Democrats by the millions fled the new, radical Democratic Party, and millions of independents and Republicans of all races joined them to elect Donald Trump president in an electoral landslide. In fact, as was noted earlier, more than 140,000 black voters in Pennsylvania provided the margin of victory for Donald Trump in that state,[371] making it possible for him to win the White House. Why did they do that? The answer is that black Americans saw Donald Trump as a different kind of presidential candidate. They didn't see him as a Republican but as an outsider. He was blunt and honest with voters. Listen to what uber-liberal movie director Michael Moore said when he predicted a Trump victory:

> When Trump stood in the shadow of a Ford Motor factory during the Michigan primary, he threatened the corporation that if they did indeed go ahead with their planned closure of that factory and move it to Mexico, he would slap a 35% tariff on any Mexican-built cars shipped back to the United

> States. It was sweet, sweet music to the ears of the working class of Michigan.... He [Trump] doesn't need Colorado or Virginia. Just Michigan, Ohio, Pennsylvania and Wisconsin. And that will put him over the top. This is how it will happen in November.[372]

Moore was precisely right: Trump was the one Republican who could and did win over the blue-collar voters, black and white, that he needed for victory in traditionally Democratic midwestern states.

Trump didn't cater to the political establishment in Washington, D.C.; he was interested only in the hardworking Americans who had been abandoned by the establishment elites on both coasts. That was one reason millions of disaffected Democrats, including nearly 1.4 million black voters,[373] flocked to support this outspoken "blue-collar billionaire."[374] Republican insiders were aghast and angry when the outsider Trump won the Republican nomination for president. They were determined to do everything possible to keep him from upsetting their business-as-usual approach. Never Trumpers left and right attacked him, but in the end, Donald John Trump was elected president of the United States thanks to the support of commonsense Americans of all races.

Once he was elected, the establishment, both Republicans and Democrats, convinced themselves that they could tame Donald Trump and make him dance to their tune. They were sure he wouldn't actually do what he'd promised. Their establishment nominees never lived up to their promises, so why should they believe that Trump would? That's why, when he was elected, both Republicans and Democrats were stunned when Trump proceeded to do exactly what he said he would do. Trump said he would put people back to work, and he did.[375] He said he would undertake policies that would lower the black unemployment rate, and he did (to the lowest recorded level in American history).[376] He said he would get them off food stamps, and he did, with food stamp recipients dropping by 3.5 million by August 2018.[377] Trump said he would ignite the economy with a tax cut, and he did, as it reached a growth rate of more than 4 percent.[378] This America first president said he would make our European allies pay their fair share of NATO costs, and for the first time they are starting to do so, increasing their contribution to NATO by $100 billion.[379] Donald Trump promised to defeat ISIS, and he did it faster than anyone thought it could be done.[380] He promised to rebuild our military, and he did.[381] During the campaign, Trump promised to move the U.S. embassy in Israel to Jerusalem, and he did.[382] Donald Trump told black Americans that he would push Congress to pass prison reform, and he did, freeing thousands of nonviolent prisoners.[383] When it came to education, he promised to deliver high-quality choice schools to poor black communities and to restore the Washington, D.C., voucher scholarship program (killed by Obama), and he has.[384]

Along the way, not only has Donald Trump made America energy independent for the first time in more than 70 years, today the United States is a net exporter of natural gas and oil.[385] Every president, Republican or Democrat, has promised energy independence since Richard Nixon, but Trump is the first to achieve it, and he did it in less than two years in office. In addition, Trump has lowered the price of energy and electricity instead of raising both as the Democrats sought to do.[386] When Trump came into office, our southern border was wide open. Criminals, gang members, those engaged in the sex slave trade, and even terrorists were coming into our nation at alarming rates. President Trump promised to end this threat to our nation and its citizens by building a wall, but both Republicans and Democrats blocked his efforts. Trump knew that the illegal entry of millions of migrants was taking jobs away from poor black Americans. He still faces great resistance from establishment politicians who are in the hip pocket of the Chamber of Commerce and Democratic radicals who seek open borders. Nevertheless, President Trump has not given in and won't give in. Through the threat of tariffs on Mexico and construction of the wall he is bringing the flood of illegal immigrants to a halt.

This president often meets with Christian leaders,[387] black and white, to better understand the problems they face in exercising their freedom of religion and to let them know he stands with them. As Vice President Pence said, *"There's prayer going on on a regular basis in this White House."*[388] Donald Trump also has proved himself to be a defender of Christians and Christianity. On the 2017 National Day of Prayer, President Trump issued an executive order to protect the rights of Christians and other people of faith in the United States who have increasingly been under attack for their religious views.[389] As Franklin Graham said of President Trump, *"He defends the Christian faith more than any president in my lifetime."*[390] Trump established a special council of Christian leaders, black and white, to meet in the White House regularly. Their purpose is to provide suggestions on how the president can protect the rights of Christians who are under attack in our land. An enemy of political correctness, Donald Trump even promised that we would be able to say "Merry Christmas" again, and we can. But every step of the way, Donald Trump had to battle not only the Democrats but also establishment Republicans, not to mention embedded Obama-era bureaucrats who sought to foil his plans for a resurgent America. He is still battling them, and he is still winning.

These are some of the reasons the stream of black voters to Donald Trump and the Republican Party continues to grow and expand. Will it be like the massive migration that occurred between 1932 and 1936 to Franklin Roosevelt, whose black support doubled in just four years? It is too soon to know if that will be true, but undoubtedly something very big is happening.

Strangely, the Democrats don't seem to care. Apparently, they are too busy courting illegal aliens and fighting against building a border wall to be concerned with the growing interest of black

Americans in Donald Trump. They are also busy supporting the rights of transsexual young men to compete in women's sports and to shower with young girls.[391] And they haven't given up on political correctness, which in their minds eclipses free speech. They want to tell us what we can say, what is acceptable, and what is not. They want to expunge the role of Christians from America's history, and they encourage their violent radical followers to harass Trump officials, congressmen, and senators they don't like in restaurants and other public places.[392] For today's radical Democrats, civilized behavior is optional.

CHAPTER 14

Going on Offense

How can conservatives and Donald Trump turn the tables on the Democrats and win over a large share of the black vote in 2020? As we know, Democrats have been successful at winning 90 to 95 percent of the black vote in election after election. They do this by labeling conservatives and Republicans as racists. It makes no difference that it is a bald-faced lie and that they are the real racists. It has worked since the racist LBJ tarred Barry Goldwater with that label, and so they're not going to stop as long as it keeps working. Nevertheless, as Trump proved in Pennsylvania in 2016, there's no reason a Republican candidate shouldn't be able to win a large share of the black vote by appealing to conservative and moderate black Americans. But to accelerate the defection of black voters from the Democratic Party, Republicans must go on offense. Going on offense doesn't mean being uncivil; it simply means telling the unfortunate truth that today's racists are progressive Democrats who support racist policies.

When attacked and called a racist, the typical response by Republicans is to go on defense and deny the charge. That does not work. Here's what happens. Each time a Republican goes on defense, it comes across to black Americans as an admission of guilt, confirming the racist label applied to Republicans by the Democrats. A Republican officeholder or candidate who pleads that he meant to give no offense or who remains silent only strengthens the belief among black Americans that all Republicans are racist.

Once the Republican plays defense, the mainstream news media pile on, using their megaphone to amplify the charge made by the Democrats that the Republican is a racist. In response, if the Republican backs down further, apologizing and backtracking, he simply reinforces the idea that he is in fact a racist. No matter the facts or the apology, the attacks don't stop. Instead, they intensify. The media dwells on the alleged incident of racism for weeks and weeks to drum it into the minds of the black community and the American public in general that this is just another case of racism by the Republicans. No war or football game was ever won by staying on defense.

In election after election, reinforced by the news media, the Democrats attack by using the false charge of racism in radio ads over black radio stations, in speeches ("*they want to put you back in chains*"[393]), and on television. The dishonest attacks then are picked up and broadcast far and wide by national television "news" broadcasts that falsely claim that all Republicans are racist. Democrats go to extremes to emphasize the idea that all Republicans are racists, running radio ads with outrageous and dishonest charges such as this ad by the Missouri Democratic Party: "*When you don't vote, you let another church explode. When you don't vote, you allow another cross to burn.*"[394] The goal, of course, is to terrorize the black community into believing that if Republicans are elected, black churches will be bombed and cross burning will return. Never mind that only Democrats have burned crosses, since only Democrats have been members of the Ku Klux Klan.

But these outrageous charges of Republican racism are going to continue until Republicans wake up and summon the necessary courage to go on offense. Again, this is not about abandoning civility or getting down in the gutter with the Democrats; it's simply about telling the truth. "*You will know the truth, and the truth will set you free.*"[395] Republican officeholders and candidates must stop cowering in the corner and instead calmly point out that it is the Democrats who are the true racists because they support racist policies and programs. Of course, it's not easy, and yes, Democrats and their lackeys in the news media won't take it lying down. But make no mistake, unless and until Republicans stand up and fight back, Democrats will continue to win a vast majority of the black vote.

The objective is to put the Democrats on defense. Remember, the Democrats must win more than 85 percent of the black vote to stay in power. If it slips just a bit to 80 percent or less, they can't win. The Democratic Party will be forced into a survival mode. Donald Trump winning more than 20 percent of the black vote in Pennsylvania[396] is a harbinger of the opportunity Republicans have to win back the black vote in 2020.

So, how does a Republican under attack go on offense? He must start by remembering that the truth is on his side. Although Democrats talk about imaginary dog whistles, Republicans can simply point out specific racist policies and programs supported by today's Democrats. It is the Democrats who have been and are truly racist because of their deeds, not the Republicans. Racism appears in the Democrats' national platform, which supports continued funding for Planned Parenthood that targets black babies for abortion, embraces the Paris Agreement that would destroy jobs for black Americans, and calls for higher prices for fossil fuels.[397] These Democratic policies are racist and are in direct opposition to the values of the black community, especially black Christians.

The bottom line is this: Republicans and conservatives must turn the tables on the Democrats when they are smeared as being racist. When a Democrat accuses or hints that a Republican is a racist, that Republican cannot cower on defense and simply plead innocence. Instead, he must courageously and immediately set the record straight, telling the truth that it is Democrats who support racist policies. GOP candidates must immediately recount the times their accusers have supported racist policies that result in the targeting of black babies for abortion, poor schools, low wages, high energy costs, and obstacles to black entrepreneurship. He must put his Democratic opponent on defense. He can justifiably show righteous outrage at being smeared as a racist but, more important, expose the progressive Democrat as the real racist. If there is any doubt about the racism of today's Democrats, just look at the governor and attorney general of the commonwealth of Virginia, who dressed in blackface and oppose policies that help black Americans.[398] Just as Republicans have never abandoned their civil rights lineage that traces back to Abraham Lincoln, Democrats have never abandoned their racist linage that traces back to the founder of their party, Andrew Jackson, and the founder of the progressive movement, Woodrow Wilson.

Today, almost anything can be racism according to politically correct liberals and their left-wing backers in the mainstream news media. If a Republican suggests a new policy that will put more poor black people in jobs and thus trim the welfare rolls, that Republican is a racist. If a black Democrat politician breaks the law or commits an immoral or unethical act and a Republican calls him out, the Republican is charged with committing racism. If a Republican supports the police, he is automatically deemed a racist when the real racist is the Democrat politician who says nothing when poor black areas become war zones where innocents die because of a lack of law and order. If you are white and you disagree with a black politician on taxes, you are called a racist.

Of course, the worst and most venomous hatred by progressive Democrats is reserved for conservative black Republicans. The attitude of Democratic radicals and their allies in the news media is that no black American can be allowed to think for himself; he *must* be a liberal Democrat. Any black American who is conservative is automatically smeared as an "Uncle Tom." However,

Candace Owens has proved that black conservatives can not only stand up to radicals but also make them turn tail and retreat.[399] She always stays on offense.

Nevertheless, the lies and smears will continue unless Trump and his followers go on offense and stay on offense. Donald Trump has done this well. He labeled the biased media as "fake news," and the label stuck. In doing this, he has driven their approval numbers down so low that only *"17% of Americans overall trust most news organizations."*[400] This is good news, because Donald Trump is right: Each day, the left-leaning media continues to spew lies and falsehoods designed to keep the president and his supporters on defense.

That's why Donald Trump is called a racist and will continue to be called a racist. The Democrats must do this to maintain their near monopoly of black votes. For Democrats and their allies in the media, winning comes first and the truth comes in a distant second. It makes no difference that as a billionaire developer Donald Trump hired scores of black Americans and placed black women such as Lynne Patton in positions of power in the Trump organization[401] or that along with Rosa Parks and Muhammad Ali, Donald Trump received the Ellis Island award for brotherhood, tolerance, and diversity.[402] No, votes and the power that comes with winning votes are all that matters to the radical left. For liberal/progressive Democrats, the end always justifies the means.

Although President Trump doesn't roll over when he is accused of being a racist, even he doesn't go far enough. He needs to tell the truth that Democrats and liberals are the real racists in our society. That is the case not because someone intentionally misinterpreted what they said but because they continue to support policies and programs that hurt black Americans. That's real racism.

When the self-proclaimed socialist Congresswoman Alexandria Ocasio-Cortez (AOC) was interviewed by Anderson Cooper (AC) on the CBS News program *60 Minutes*,[403] it was a typical liberal echo chamber with a left-wing politician being asked softball questions by an equally left-wing "journalist." The portion of the interview dealing with the "racism" of Donald Trump went like this:

> **AOC:** The president certainly didn't invent racism. But he's certainly given a voice to it and expanded it and created a platform for those things,
>
> **AC:** Do you believe President Trump is a racist?
>
> **AOC:** Yeah, no question.
>
> **AC:** How can you say that?
>
> **AOC:** When you look at the words that he uses, which are historic dog whistles of white supremacy. When you look at how he reacted to the Charlottesville incident, where neo-Nazis murdered a woman, versus how he manufactures crises like immigrants seeking legal refuge on our borders, it's—it's night and day.

Of course, there was no follow-up question, nor did Anderson Cooper point out that Richard Spencer, the organizer of the Charlottesville event, is an advocate of a powerful centralized government who dislikes Ronald Reagan and dislikes America's Founders but admires the slaveholding founder of the Democratic Party, Andrew Jackson.[404] And of course there was no discussion of issues such as Trump policies that have created the lowest black and Hispanic unemployment rate in recorded history.[405] No mention, of course, of the First Step Act criminal justice reform measure signed by President Trump that has set many black non-violent inmates free.[406]

This interview is another good example of how the liberals rig the system. Notice that Ocasio-Cortez never pointed out any acts of real racism such as actually supporting racist policies that hurt black or Hispanic Americans. Ocasio-Cortez didn't do that because there aren't any. Not one. The Democrats use this tactic repeatedly, citing no policies, just "dog whistles," and the mainstream media never challenge them.

This is what White House Press Secretary Sarah Sanders said when President Trump was attacked by Alexandria Ocasio-Cortez: *"Congresswoman Ocasio-Cortez's sheer ignorance on the matter can't cover the fact that President Trump supported and passed historic criminal justice reform"* and *"has repeatedly condemned racism and bigotry in all forms."*[407]

That response is good as far as it goes, but Sanders should have gone on offense, pointing out that the Democratic Party, of which Ocasio-Cortez is a member, advocates racist policies. She would have better served the president with a response similar to this one:

> Not only is President Trump not a racist, but the fact is that Miss Ocasio-Cortez belongs to a party that supports racist policies that hurt black and Hispanic citizens. They block high-quality schools for poor black and Hispanic families; they slavishly back Planned Parenthood, a group that systematically targets unborn black babies for abortion; they also callously favor raising the price of heating fuel and gasoline, which disproportionately hurts poor black families; they seek open borders that not only flood the market with cheap illegal labor, taking jobs away from poor blacks and Hispanics, but also increase the flow of illegal drugs into their communities. Worse, this policy allows dangerous MS-13 members to terrorize the same poor families. If that's not a pattern of racism, then I don't know what is.

That kind of statement would have put the news media and the Democrats on defense, but the press secretary played defense instead of offense. President Trump brushed Ocasio-Cortez off, which is appropriate for a president talking about a freshman congresswoman, but there is no excuse for the White House press secretary not going on offense. Conservatives and Republicans have nothing to be embarrassed about or apologetic about. Conservative Republicans are the ones who have always been faithful to the legacy of President Abraham Lincoln, whereas progressive Democrats have remained racist throughout their history.

Until conservative Republicans start going on offense and point out the racist policies of liberal/progressive Democrats, they will never win a large share of the black vote. They will never create a flood of black Americans to the Republican Party. It's not only a matter of courage; it's about telling the truth.

CHAPTER 15

Coming Home

Whether in a stream or a river, black Americans are leaving the Democratic Party to join the party of Donald J. Trump. When did this exodus begin? It didn't start this year, 5 years ago, or even 10 years ago. In reality, it started in the late 1980s and early 1990s as a tiny trickle of black Americans that included Vernon Robinson and others who realized that the Democratic Party had left them. But who are these black patriots who are now leaving liberalism and the Democratic Party in greater numbers each year?

For the most part, this is a youth movement, a migration of young black Americans to the banner of President Trump, just as was the migration of black Americans to the banner of FDR in the 1930s. This is a new generation of black Americans, educated, upwardly mobile, professional, and tired of the broken promises of the Democratic Party. It is also the first generation of black Americans who did not experience the horrors and dangers of progressive segregation or the nearly universal attitude among white Americans that they were superior to black Americans. Yes, they heard the stories, but to them it is like ancient history. This movement to Donald Trump also was made possible by the fact that today nearly 52 percent of black Americans are economically in the middle class and 3 percent are in the upper class.[408] The working poor category accounts for 25 percent, and those in poverty receiving government assistance are 21.2 percent of the total.[409] For young, upwardly mobile black Americans, their concerns aren't economic survival, racism, and personal danger but rather personal achievement and upward economic growth.

It's not that there weren't conservative black Americans before 1990, such as George Schuyler, who wrote the book *Black and Conservative* in 1966.[410] It's just that there were virtually no conservative black elected officials, conservative black candidates for president, high-profile conservative black entertainers, conservative black sports stars, black conservative commentators, black conservative authors, conservative black professors, or black conservatives on television and radio as there are today. And today, no matter what part of our society you look at, you inevitably will find black Americans moving up the ladder of influence and economic success.

This migration to Trump, which eventually will lead to a migration to the Republican Party, began as a tiny, almost invisible stream. One of the very first signs of black departure from the Democratic plantation were books and newspaper columns by professors Walter Williams and Thomas Sowell as well as a few black young conservatives who joined Young Americans for Freedom in the 1960s. Of course, the 1991 nomination of Clarence Thomas to the U.S. Supreme Court was an eye-opening event for black Americans. Democrats made the mistake of mercilessly attacking Thomas, and it backfired. Black Americans were shocked by the disgusting effort of Democrats to destroy Thomas. For his part, Thomas characterized the Democrats' effort as a *"high tech lynching."*[411] Black Americans witnessed Republicans staunchly defending Thomas even as the Democratic attacks on him continued and intensified. In spite of the Democrats' attacks on Clarence Thomas, 70 percent of black Americans stood with him.[412] This was undoubtedly a watershed moment that caused many black Americans, especially younger black Americans, to question their loyalty to the Democratic Party.

Then, as time passed and cable TV grew and expanded, more black Americans began to appear on television, including conservatives such as Jason Riley of the *Wall Street Journal* and Charles Payne of the Fox Business Channel. Then businessman Herman Cain made a strong run for the Republican nomination for president in 2012, followed by Dr. Ben Carson in 2016. Along the way, unseen and unnoticed by television or the mainstream media, conservative black Americans all across the nation began to run for public office, host local call-in radio shows, and write books and blogs. They ran for the U.S. House of Representatives and the U.S. Senate; they ran for the city council, for mayor, for the county council, and for the state legislature. The number of black conservative candidates continued to grow and expand. They ran in increasing numbers, and inevitably they began to win elections to local office, to the state legislature, to statewide offices, and even to Congress.

The list of black conservative leaders that follows includes just a very few of the hundreds or even thousands of conservative black Americans who are serving in public office, heading up conservative organizations, holding forth on TV, writing for influential publications, serving in powerful appointed positions, writing books and blogs, and even, like Kanye West and Stacey Dash, performing in the entertainment industry. Today large numbers of black voters cast their votes for conservative Republican candidates at every level of government.

How big is the migration of black Americans back to the party of Abraham Lincoln and Donald Trump? That is difficult to know because a large number of middle-class black Americans have moved to the suburbs. These more conservative black voters are spread out and intermingled with middle-class whites, Hispanics, and Asian Americans, making it costly and difficult to find out how they vote. In fact, it is highly likely that in 2016 the black vote for Donald Trump was significantly undercounted. Not only were middle-class black Americans difficult to find, when they were found, they were understandably reluctant to tell a stranger over the telephone that they planned to vote for Donald Trump. Accordingly, the black vote for Trump in 2016 in Pennsylvania was probably 25 percent or more. Nevertheless, even using an estimate of 8 percent support, nearly 1.4 million black Americans nationally voted for Donald Trump for president in 2016.[413]

No matter how you look at it, the tide has turned, thanks in large part to Donald Trump. If you doubt that is true, take a quick look at the following list of black conservative stars—political officeholders, political candidates, book authors, talk show hosts, television contributors, television hosts, podcast hosts, intellectuals, political appointees, political activists, entertainers, and actors:

- Renee Amoore, deputy chair of Pennsylvania GOP, member of Trump transition team
- Christopher Arps, director of Move-On-Up.org
- Deana Bass, press secretary for Ben Carson's 2016 presidential campaign
- Ashley D. Bell, southeastern regional administrator for the Small Business Administration
- Walter Blackman, 2018 Arizona state representative
- Ken Blackwell, former Ohio treasurer and secretary of state, Trump transition team
- Deneen Borelli, author, Fox News Channel contributor, FreedomWorks outreach director
- Rhetta Bowers, 2018 Texas House of Representatives
- Mark Burns, televangelist, spoke at 2016 Republican National Convention
- Jineea Butler, 2010 candidate for Congress, 13th District, New York
- Herman Cain, former chairman and CEO of Godfather's Pizza, 2012 presidential candidate, Fox News Channel contributor
- Gianno Caldwell, Fox News political analyst

- Jennifer Carroll, lieutenant governor of Florida
- Ben Carson, world-renowned brain surgeon, 2016 presidential candidate, secretary of HUD
- Stefani Carter, Texas House of Representatives
- Ron Christie, adviser to Vice President Dick Cheney
- Matt Clement, conservative podcaster
- Ward Connerly, president of American Civil Rights Institute
- Horace Cooper, co-chairman, Project 21 National Advisory Board
- Frank Cousins, first African-American sheriff in Massachusetts
- Stacey Dash, actress, Fox News Channel commentator
- Artur Davis, former Alabama Democratic congressman
- Paris Dennard, aide to George W. Bush, CNN and NPR contributor
- Wayne Dupree, talk radio host, founder of We Are America Radio network
- Larry Elder, lawyer, talk show host, Fox News Channel contributor, author
- James Evans, Utah State Senate, chairman of Utah Republican Party
- Jose Evans, Indianapolis City Council, ran for mayor of Indianapolis
- Melvin Everson, former member of Georgia House of Representatives
- Michael Faulkner, World Vision Director of Programs, Pastor, New Horizon Church, played for New York Jets (1981–1982), 2010 congressional candidate
- George Ferrell, chairman of BlakPac
- Ada Fisher, MD, Republican national committeewoman from North Carolina
- Gary Franks, past member of U.S. House of Representatives for Connecticut
- James Garner, mayor of Village of Hempstead, New York

- Darryl Glenn, 2016 candidate for U.S. Senate from Colorado
- James Golden, aka "Bo Snerdley," producer of Rush Limbaugh radio show
- Phillip Goudeaux, pastor of Calvary Christian Center, Sacramento, California
- Elbert Guillory, Louisiana House and Senate, YouTube video with 1.4 million views
- Jenean Hampton, lieutenant governor of Kentucky, 2015
- Caleb L. Hanna, West Virginia delegate, youngest in United States, elected 2018
- Ineitha Hardaway, "Diamond" of Diamond and Silk
- Erika Harold, 2003 Miss America, 2012 candidate for U.S. Congress, 2018 candidate for Illinois attorney general
- Curtis Hill, 43rd attorney general of Indiana
- Mike Hill, Florida House of Representatives
- Amy Holmes, political commentator, independent social conservative
- Deborah Honeycutt, 2006, 2008, 2010 congressional candidate
- Peggy Hubbard, 2020 candidate for U.S. Senate from Illinois, 700,000 YouTube views
- Will Hurd, U.S. representative from Texas, former CIA analyst
- Lynn Hutchings, Wyoming House of Representatives
- Niger Innis, commentator, author, activist
- Carl Jackson, columnist, Townhall
- E. W. Jackson, 2013 candidate for lieutenant governor of Virginia, Harvard Law graduate, founder of S.T.A.N.D.
- Kevin Jackson, talk radio host, Fox News Channel contributor, author
- Raynard Jackson, political analyst for WUSA*9 TV (CBS), Washington, D.C.
- Conrad James, New Mexico House of Representatives

- John James, combat veteran, 2018 and 2020 candidate for U.S. Senate from Michigan
- Kay Cole James, president of Heritage Foundation, worked in administrations of George H.W. Bush and George Bush, as well as cabinet position in administration of Virginia Governor Allen, former Dean of Robertson School of Government at Regent University
- Wallace B. Jefferson, chief justice of Supreme Court of Texas
- Dwayne "The Rock" Johnson, Hollywood star and former professional wrestler
- Sonnie Johnson, "Did She Say That with Sonnie Johnson" podcast
- C. Robert Jones, PhD, "The Dr. C. Robert Jones Situation Report" podcast
- Lawrence Jones, editor in chief of Campus Reform, Fox News Channel contributor
- Alan Keyes, U.S. ambassador, candidate for U.S. Senate in Maryland and Illinois
- Alveda King, minister, author, former state legislator in Georgia
- Don King, boxing promoter, stumped for Trump in 2016
- Stephen N. Lackey, fundraiser and philanthropist
- Jim Lawrence, former member of New Hampshire House of Representatives
- Willie Lawson, "REAL TALK" podcast
- Bruce LeVell, executive director of National Diversity Coalition for Trump in 2016
- Leah LeVell, leader of RNC African-American Initiatives and Urban Media team
- Nic Lott, chairman of Mississippi Young Republicans, College Republicans
- Aisha Love, executive director of Black Women Walk
- Telly Lovelace, former national director of black initiatives, RNC

- Julian Lowe, pastor of Oasis Church, Los Angeles
- Leo Mackay, Jr., deputy secretary of Department of Veterans Affairs
- Karl Malone, former NBA star, member of NBA Hall of Fame
- Kenneth Mapp, governor of U.S. Virgin Islands
- Lenny McAllister, TV and radio host, author, 2013 Pennsylvania congressional candidate
- Angela McGlowan, political analyst, 2010 Mississippi congressional candidate
- Clarence McKee, has influenced GOP platform since Ronald Reagan
- Ron Miller, communications director in Calvert County, Maryland, GOP
- Van Moody, pastor of Worship Center Christian Church in Montgomery, Alabama
- Deroy Murdock, columnist, TV contributor
- Right Reverend Council Nedd II, PhD, founding member of Project 21
- Sophia A. Nelson, lawyer, author, political commentator
- Samuel Newby, Jacksonville City Council, former chairman of Duval County GOP
- Constance Newman, former assistant secretary of state for African affairs
- Candace Owens, former director of communications for Turning Point USA
- Rod Paige, U.S. secretary of education
- Vernon Parker, mayor of Paradise Valley, Arizona, 2010 congressional candidate
- Lynne Patton, VP, Eric Trump Foundation, YouTube video with 5 million views, head of Region II of HUD
- Charles Payne, *Making Money with Charles Payne*, Fox News Channel
- Edward J. Perkins, first black U.S. ambassador to South Africa, Reagan appointee

- Jesse Lee Peterson, civil rights activist, founder of Brotherhood of a New Destiny
- Joseph C. Phillips, writer, columnist, TV and radio commentator
- Katrina Pierson, national spokeswoman for Trump 2016 campaign
- Jon Ponder, pastor and CEO of Hope for Prisoners, Las Vegas
- Jane E. Powdrell-Culbert, 2018 New Mexico House of Representatives
- Michael Powell, 24th chairman of FCC, president of National Cable & Telecommunications Association
- Joe Profit, Atlanta Falcons, candidate for U.S. House of Representatives in Georgia
- Shannon Reeves, past RNC national director, state and local development
- Condoleezza Rice, 66th U.S. secretary of state, Hoover Institution
- Herneitha Richardson, "Silk" of Diamond and Silk
- Jason Riley, Manhattan Institute, *Wall Street Journal* and Fox News Channel contributor, author
- Samuel Rivers, Jr., South Carolina House of Representatives
- Vernon Robinson, former Winston-Salem councilman, political director of Ben Carson super PAC
- Joe Rogers, lieutenant governor of Colorado, youngest in state history
- Carson Ross, mayor of Blue Springs, Missouri, former state representative
- Boyd Rutherford, lieutenant governor of Maryland
- Elroy Sailor, 2016 Trump transition team
- Dwayne Sawyer, state auditor, Indiana
- Darrell Scott, Cleveland, Ohio, pastor, 2016 Trump transition team
- Marvin Scott, PhD, former assistant dean of graduate studies, School of Education, Butler University, 2010

congressional candidate, 2004 U.S. Senate candidate from Indiana

- Tim Scott, former congressman, current U.S. senator from South Carolina
- Gloreatha "Glo" Scurry-Smith, 2016 U.S. House candidate from Florida
- Kyle Searcy, bishop and pastor at Fresh Anointing House of Worship, Montgomery, Alabama
- Winsome Sears, Virginia delegate 2004, congressional candidate, chair of Black Americans to Re-Elect the President
- Tara Setmayer, CNN political commentator
- T. W. Shannon, speaker of Oklahoma House of Representatives
- Leo J. Smith, state director of minority engagement of Georgia GOP
- Princella Smith, 2010 congressional candidate, ShePAC member
- Rob Smith, Turning Point USA spokesman, U.S. Army veteran
- Thomas Sowell, author, economist, senior fellow at Hoover Institution
- Shelby Steele, author, columnist, senior fellow at Hoover Institution
- Thomas Stith III, former city councilman in Durham, North Carolina, chief of staff for Governor Pat McCrory 2013–2017
- Carol M. Swain, author, professor at Vanderbilt University
- Lynn Swann, NFL star, former candidate for governor of Pennsylvania
- Willie Talton, former member of Georgia General Assembly
- Ashley Taylor, attorney, former deputy attorney general of Virginia
- Arthur Teele, assistant secretary of transportation
- Clarence Thomas, Associate Justice, U.S. Supreme Court, author

- Thurman Thomas, Buffalo Bills, Republican activist
- Maj Toure, founder of Black Guns Matter
- Scott Turner, Texas House of Representatives
- Jill Upson, West Virginia House of Delegates, 2012, 2014
- Dale Wainwright, associate justice, Texas Supreme Court
- J. C. Watts, former U.S. representative from Oklahoma
- Stacy Washington, co-chair of Project 21 National Advisory Board, host of *Stacy on the Right*
- David Webb, talk show host, *Reality Check with David Webb*
- Allen West, former U.S. Representative from Florida
- Kanye West, entrepreneur, rapper, singer, songwriter, fashion designer
- James White, Texas House of Representatives
- Alvin Williams, executive director of Black America's PAC
- Armstrong Williams, radio and television commentator
- Jeffrey L. Williams, president of Republicans for Black Empowerment
- Michael Williams, Texas Railroad Commission
- Raffi Williams, deputy assistant director of HUD
- David Wilson, former member of Wasilla city council, Alaska state senator
- Marvin Winans, Jr., pastor, gospel singer, Perfecting Church, Detroit,
- Jackie Winters, Oregon State Senate
- Robert Woodson, president of National Center for Neighborhood Enterprise
- LaMetta Wynn, former mayor of Clinton, Iowa

This list is incomplete, and the authors apologize to the black leaders who were inadvertently left off it. But frankly, 30 or even 20 years ago, a list like this would have contained no more than 10 or 15 names. This list is just a small sample of black conservative leaders across the nation. Today, there are legions of black conservative writers, columnists, talk show hosts, pastors, businessmen and -women, speakers, actors, candidates for public office, political activists, professors, and more. Along with these leaders there are several million black conservatives across the nation, and their number is growing daily.

This is the way that all great and successful political movements start, with people of great character, powerful ideas, and a firm commitment and determination to make America better. Can the day be far away when the number of black Republicans in Congress equals or exceeds the number of black Democrats? It is finally possible to imagine 20 or even 30 percent of the black vote going to conservative Republican candidates. That could even happen for Donald Trump in 2020.

The truth is that although they are still far from becoming a majority, conservative black Republicans have momentum on their side in politics, in ideas, in churches, and even in the media. After all, the belief that one political party can reliably count on getting the votes of 90 to 95 percent of any voting bloc over a long period is simply foolhardy. Liberal Democrats know that their views are 180 degrees out of phase with those of many black Americans. That's why the Democrats' screams of racism have become so frantic and unhinged. Although the Democrat leadership is confident that it can simply sit back in 2020 and count on the black vote by calling Donald Trump a racist, that sick lie is running out of gas.

Although Franklin Roosevelt did not win the black vote in 1932, he and his team focused on winning it in 1936. On September 22, 1936, more than 16,000 black Americans rallied at Madison Square Garden in New York City to celebrate Emancipation Day and support Franklin D. Roosevelt.[414] It is noteworthy that the event's sponsor, the Good Neighbor League, established a special committee to host the event that consisted almost exclusively of former Republicans.[415] This large rally signaled a mass exodus of black Americans from the Republican Party to the Democratic Party. A similar seminal event took place on January 20, 2019, when a huge Blexit (Black Exit from the Democratic Party) rally was held in Los Angeles, California.[416] Although smaller than the 1936 event in New York City on behalf of FDR, this big rally celebrated the exit of black Americans from the Democratic Party to support Donald Trump in 2020. More than a thousand black former Democrats enthusiastically celebrated their escape from the Democratic Party of handouts to the Republican Party of opportunity and prosperity. Similar to the reaction of Republican bigwigs in 1936, the Democrat politicians yawned and dismissed this event as a nonhappening, even though similar rallies in other big U.S. cities were announced that night.[417]

One person who attended the event was Joy Villa, a conservative black and Hispanic singer/songwriter, who said, *"What changed my mind is being disillusioned with the Democratic Party. I thought, 'Oh yeah, I'm going to be a part of this system that is supposed to help me and my people.' And I realized, it does not help anybody."*[418]

Those in attendance at the rally wore T-shirts and hats with slogans such as "BLEXIT," "Make America Great Again," and perhaps most poignantly, "Liberals Can't Bully Me." There was plenty of enthusiasm, optimism, and energy at this upbeat event about leaving the Democratic plantation, but few in the Democratic Party took notice.[419] Coverage by the liberal mainstream media was nearly nonexistent.

The departure of black Americans from the Republican Party in 1936 can't be denied, nor can the departure of black Americans from the Democratic Party today. As in 1936, when the loyalty of black Americans leaving the Republican Party was limited to Franklin Roosevelt, today the loyalty of those leaving the Democratic Party is primarily limited to Donald Trump. Remember, it was not until 1948, 16 years after FDR first ran and won the White House, that more black Americans identified as Democrats than as Republicans.[420]

But this remigration to the party of Abraham Lincoln and Donald Trump won't continue to grow and expand in a vacuum. It needs nurturing and encouragement.

CHAPTER 16

Organizing for Victory

There are two substantial challenges to winning 20 percent or more of the black vote for Donald Trump in 2020. The first is, as was noted earlier, rebuilding trust with black Americans. The second is a reliable way of communicating the truth to black Americans that conservatives truly care about them and want the best for them while also reminding them that the new radical Democrats have values that are antithetical to their own. Thanks to the biased news media, most black Americans do not realize that conservatives are truly in political harmony with the goals and objectives of most black Americans.

The reality is that the liberal news media and the Democrats have for decades successfully isolated black Americans from the truth about Republicans and conservatives in general. Even in public school textbooks, the word *conservative* is outrageously equated to racism.[421] One textbook for advanced placement students that is used all across America *"describes Trump as mentally ill"*[422] and his supporters as racist. In other words, schoolchildren from grade school to college are falsely taught that racist and conservative are one and the same, and accordingly, that Donald Trump and all conservatives are racist.

But it's more than that. Democrats have never told the truth about their own history as slaveholders and the creators of Jim Crow segregation[423] or their current opposition to quality schools for black children as well as their support for Planned Parenthood, which targets black babies for abortion.[424] In fact, a poll taken by The Polling Company, revealed the following:[425]

- By a margin of 80 percent to 9 percent, black Americans believe Democrats, not Republicans, would be more helpful to *"men and women who want to be small business owners."*
- By a margin of 62 percent to 19 percent, black voters believe Democrats are likelier than Republicans to *"reduce crime by jailing violent criminals."*
- By a margin of 75 percent to 11 percent, black Americans believe Democrats are likelier than Republicans to *"lower taxes."*
- 62 percent of black Americans believe Democrats are likelier than Republicans *"to reduce terrorism by strengthening the national defense."*
- By the wide margin of 69 percent to 13 percent, black Americans said that Democrats, not Republicans, would *"protect the rights of unborn children."*

Although this poll is more than 15 years old, it shows just how effective the Democrats and the mainstream media have been in covering up the actual record of the Democratic Party. Because of the demonization of Republicans and the lack of communication from Republicans, black voters ascribe policy positions they agree with to Democrats and policy positions they disagree with to Republicans.

A good example of isolation from conservative ideas and progressive views is the nearly total absence of black viewers of the Fox News Channel (FNC). Although FNC is consistently the most watched cable news network in America, the fact is that only 1 percent of its audience is black.[426] This further explains why black Americans don't know that historically Democrats always raise taxes and Republicans cut them. They don't know that whereas Republicans support black entrepreneurship, Democrats favor more business-killing regulations and other roadblocks that keep black Americans from going into business. Black Americans don't know that Democrats are always soft on crime and terrorism, whereas Republicans are tough on these life-threatening issues. Most shocking of all, black Americans don't even know that Democrats are pro-abortion whereas Republicans and conservatives are pro-life. No wonder Republican candidates receive few votes from black Americans. That makes the exodus of black voters, especially younger black voters, to Donald Trump even more stunning and amazing.

Make no mistake, politically savvy Democrats are terrified that black Americans are leaving their party. Trump's overtures to black Americans scare them to death. It's no wonder they have escalated their smears, now calling Donald Trump not only a racist but even a *"white supremacist."*[427] They will do anything to stop these voters from escaping to Donald Trump. Democratic attacks on Republicans and lies about Donald Trump are sure to intensify as the 2020 election nears. In fact, let's not forget that one of the most racist presidents in history, Lyndon Johnson, was willing to do something he loathed—give full rights to black Americans in the 1964 Civil Rights Bill and the 1965 Voting Rights Act—to hold on to the black vote. Like Johnson, the new socialist Democrats of today are determined to win at any cost.

The good news is that in spite of having the deck stacked against him, Donald Trump has a unique opportunity in 2020. Just like the Republicans in 1936, the Democrats are confident that they own the black vote. They simply can't imagine Donald Trump winning a significant amount of the black vote in 2020. That means that now is the time to strike. And there is a strategy to do just that. Let's start with the trust issue.

How does President Trump continue to build trust with black Americans? The Democrats have had great success eradicating any trust that black Americans might have had in the Republican Party or its candidates, but Donald Trump does not carry all the typical Republican and conservative baggage. He hasn't been a Washington, D.C., insider; he has spent his life in the business world. Nevertheless, building trust after decades of suspicion by black Americans and disregard of black Americans by Republicans is not an easy task.

Consider how hard it was for Dr. Ben Carson to move from the Democratic Party to the Republican Party. In his book *America the Beautiful*, Carson explains why he didn't vote for Ronald Reagan when he ran against Jimmy Carter in 1980: *"Although Reagan's logical approach to many of our social and international problems appealed to me, he was a Republican. Because of my bias in favor of the Democratic Party, I figured Reagan must, by definition, be greedy, selfish, and callous toward the poor."*[428]

Ben Carson was very distrustful of all Republicans. He agreed with what Reagan had to say but believed the Democratic lie that Ronald Reagan was an evil racist. Thus, in spite of the fact that Carson was more in sync with the views of Reagan than he was with the views of Carter, he voted for Jimmy Carter. That is exactly where many black Americans are today. This is the challenge that Donald Trump faces in 2020. Fortunately, Ben Carson eventually learned the truth: *"As I got to know more Republicans and conservatives, however, I came to realize that many of my political beliefs were based on nothing other than propaganda, and that there were just as many decent Republicans as there were decent Democrats."*[429]

Listen to what Dr. Carson is saying. As he got to know Republicans and conservatives, he realized that he had believed a lie. So many black Americans, perhaps a majority, are in agreement with Donald Trump on the issues, but until they trust the president, they will not be able to bring themselves to vote for him in 2020.

How is Donald Trump building trust among black Americans? He is taking a page out of Franklin Roosevelt's playbook. Remember, in 1932 the image of the Democratic Party in the eyes of black Americans was far worse than that of the Republicans today. Democrats had been the slaveholders, they had instigated segregation, and they had blocked every civil rights bill or amendment put before Congress since 1865. Democrats weren't trusted by black Americans, and understandably so. Wisely, Franklin D. Roosevelt didn't ask black Americans to support the Democratic Party; he asked them to support him. He knew that asking black Americans to support the Democratic Party would prove fruitless. Instead, Roosevelt portrayed himself as a new Democrat, someone willing to work with and for black Americans. In 1932 Roosevelt made some overtures to the black community, but in 1936 he made an all-out effort to win the black vote, spending both time and money to win black support. He, his wife, and members of his inner circle met with black leaders, but Republican nominee Alf Landon did not. As we know, Roosevelt's efforts paid off handsomely. In 1936, FDR won the black vote overwhelmingly. It is unlikely that Trump will be able to match the success of FDR thanks to the dishonest news media, but the opportunity is still there to take major strides toward winning over as much as 25 to 30 percent of the black vote, especially in key swing states. If Trump does that, not only will he win the White House, he will accelerate the exodus of black Americans from the Democratic Party to the Republican Party.

Donald Trump benefits from being a nonestablishment outsider. He wasn't elected president because he was a traditional Republican but because he promised to end business as usual in Washington, D.C. Remember, he was a Democrat for most of his adult life. Trump was a highly visible billionaire businessman, a flamboyant developer, and a television superstar. In regard to his TV star status, it is important to note that black Americans made up a significant proportion of the viewership of his hit show, *The Apprentice.*[430] In fact, Donald Trump was *"very popular with Hispanic and African-American viewers of 'The Apprentice,'"* even *"more popular than he was with white viewers."*[431] All this enabled Donald Trump to start out with strong favorability from black Americans. As Jason Riley put it in the *Wall Street Journal*, "*When Donald Trump decided to run for president as a Republican, he already had a standing with black America that most GOP politicians can only dream of.*"[432] Like FDR before him, Donald Trump is working hard to establish a positive relationship with black Americans. To the extent that he acquires the trust of black voters, as Roosevelt succeeded in doing in 1936, the black vote for Donald Trump in 2020 will surge significantly, as it did for FDR.

To win back the trust of black Americans, Donald Trump is making it clear to them that he is on the same page they are. By championing the First Step Act that sets many young black non-violent prisoners free, working for quality schools in poor black areas, and initiating Opportunity Zones,[433] Trump is providing concrete evidence that he cares about black Americans.

But this must be reinforced face-to-face on the ground. One of the most powerful ways to do this was illustrated by 170 Trump supporters who went into one of the worst areas of Baltimore, cleaned it up, and hauled away nearly 12 tons of trash.[434] The people living there expressed their thanks to the volunteers and to President Trump for calling their terrible situation to the attention of the national news media.[435] This is how Republicans can prove to black Americans that they are the real friends of the black community. Furthermore, if conservative Republicans would do this across the nation on a repeated basis, it might indeed be possible for Donald Trump to win 20 percent, 30 percent, or even more of the black vote in 2020.

On another front, community organizers of the Black Americans to Re-Elect the President super PAC will be going into the black community, especially into black evangelical churches, volunteering and offering to help in any way they can. Some of these conservative community organizers will be black military veterans who know how to get things done and already have direct ties to the black community. Working with black church leaders and other black leaders on issues of urgent concern to residents of black communities, they will build personal relationships with local residents by helping black mothers fight for high-quality choice schools for their children. Working through the black churches, they will organize resistance to abortion and Planned Parenthood and to raising the price of energy. They also will coalesce opposition to open borders and the invasion of unskilled foreign illegals who take black jobs and drive down wages. These community organizers will make sure that black voters understand that Democrats are on the wrong side of these issues and are hurting black Americans.

Being a conservative community organizer in poor black areas is a demanding and difficult assignment, but such efforts prove the compassion and love Trump supporters have for their brothers and sisters. But this is only one aspect of the plan to restore trust in the black community and win black votes for Donald Trump in 2020. Pro-Trump super PACs, the Republican Party, and the official Trump campaign must make sure that black voters know that today's Democratic Party is the real home of racism in America. That's why groups such as the Republican Party of Orlando, Florida, plan to establish a satellite office within their black community as a base for passing out brochures like the one shown in the Appendix of this book. This mass distribution of literature explaining what Donald Trump has done for black Americans mirrors the efforts of Franklin Roosevelt supporters in 1936 who not only *"distributed hundreds of thousands of pieces of campaign literature"* describing *"the impact of the New Deal on blacks"*[436] but also passed out *"more than a million photographs of Mrs. Roosevelt in the company of blacks at Howard University"*[437] to reinforce the commitment of the Roosevelt administration to black Americans.

The late Richard Nadler, who was mentioned earlier, realized that a large number of black Americans were just as conservative as white Americans. Accordingly, he made it his passion in life to find a way to win over the black vote for conservative Republican candidates. In 2002, Nadler conducted an extensive meta-study of the impact of radio advertising directed at black voters. Why radio advertising? Black Americans are unique in that just as recent Hispanic immigrants listen to Spanish-language radio stations, black Americans listen to so-called black radio stations. In fact, 62 percent of all black Americans listen to an urban contemporary black radio station at least once a week.[438] This presents an avenue for reaching out directly to black Americans.

As was noted earlier, Nadler was well aware of a number of surveys that had been conducted over the years showing that approximately one-third of black Americans were in full agreement with white conservatives on key issues of the day such as taxes, abortion, national security, the national debt, and jobs. But the barrage of lies from the Democrats and the liberal news media kept them from voting for conservative Republican candidates with whom they agreed on the issues.

In 2020, there is a unique opportunity for Donald Trump to reach these black Americans because of the growing fissure between black Americans and the Democratic Party. It also helps that younger black voters no longer rely on mainstream news magazines and newspapers but instead get their news online. Thus, they are better informed, having access to a broader array of news sources. Moreover, these younger black Americans do not have the depth of commitment to the Democratic Party that their parents and grandparents had. The challenge is to reach this group and reinforce the truth that Donald Trump is their ally, at the same time reminding them that Democrats see them only as pawns to be moved on their chess board.

The 2002 meta-study conducted by Richard Nadler compared test results in 19 districts across five states comparing black support for Republican candidates in the area where radio ads were heard with the same areas that did not hear any radio ads in 2000. Although this created many variables (different candidates, different turnout, different issues, etc.), making absolute confirmation of performance statistically impossible, in 19 out of 19 black areas the black vote for the Republican candidate in 2002 increased over the vote for the Republican candidate in 2000. The average increase in the proportion of the black vote was 3.16 percentage points.[439]

As further confirmation of the success of such radio advertising, the National Draft Ben Carson for President Committee conducted a test in the 2014 North Carolina U.S. Senate race to confirm the effectiveness of advertising on black radio stations. The Senate race pitted challenger Thom Tillis against incumbent Kay Hagan. Six years earlier, Republican incumbent Elizabeth Dole received just 1 percent of the black vote in a losing race against Hagan. Two months before Election Day 2014, Thom Tillis seemed destined to experience the same fate, with polls showing that he too would win only 1 percent of the black vote.[440] But six weeks before the 2014 election, radio ads placed by the National Draft Ben Carson for President Committee began to run on a daily basis.[441] Not surprisingly, the black vote for Tillis began to climb steadily. By election day, Tillis won 11 percent of the black vote statewide[442] even though, because of financial limitations, the ads did not run in the northern crescent or the southern tier of North Carolina, where there is a heavy concentration of black voters. It appears likely that Tillis actually won 18 percent of the black vote in the areas of the state where the radio ads were run. What is known is that the increase in the black vote for Tillis provided his margin of victory.[443]

Similarly, in the last presidential election, the 2016 Committee super PAC ran an extensive radio campaign aimed at black Americans in Pennsylvania.[444] They and the official Trump campaign also reached out to black Americans with social media advertising. The result, as was previously noted, was that 21 percent of black voters in Pennsylvania (140,000+)[445] voted for President Trump, providing him with his margin of victory in that crucial state. The 2016 Committee also ran radio advertising and social media campaigns in North Carolina, Missouri, Michigan, and Wisconsin, significantly boosting the black vote in each instance.[446]

In 2018, three super PACs—Stars & Stripes Forever, Americas PAC, and Black Americans for the President's Agenda—ran radio ads in key House and Senate races;[447] again, the black vote for the Republican candidate increased significantly. It is noteworthy that the three PACs spent in excess of $1 million on radio ads in key states in 2018, increasing the black vote enough for Republicans to pick up two U.S. Senate seats.[448] The impact of this radio blitz was especially evident in Missouri, where all three super PACs ran ads for Josh Hawley and against Claire McCaskill in the U.S. Senate race. Thanks to those ads, Hawley more than doubled black voter support compared with the GOP candidate in 2012.[449] Moreover, those black voters who could not yet bring themselves to vote for a Republican chose not to vote. It was only the trust issue that kept Hawley from winning 20 percent or more of the black vote. As such advertising continues and intensifies, those black Americans who did not vote vote for the Republican candidate will find their way to the Republican Party as they learn that it is Republicans who save black babies and Democrats who advocate aborting black babies and selling their body parts.[450] Similarly, in Tennessee, where Americas PAC ran five weeks of ads on urban contemporary radio stations, Marsha Blackburn doubled her black voter support from 7 percent to 14 percent by Election Day.[451]

Donald Trump can win again in 2020 by building trust with black voters and appealing directly to them via speeches in black communities, social media communications, door-to-door contact by volunteers, and advertising on black radio stations. This will not only bring victory but also help accelerate the exodus of black Americans to the Republican Party from the Democratic Party. After all, conservative Republicans like Donald Trump are the true historic heirs of the legacy of Abraham Lincoln.

APPENDIX

What You Can Do

If you are active in the Republican Party, plan on running for office, or have been asked to serve as the chairman of a campaign, this is written for you. In the book you just finished you learned about the racial history of the Democratic and Republican parties as well as about how the Democrats persuaded black Americans to switch from the party of Lincoln to the party of Roosevelt. You also learned that black Americans are giving Donald Trump and other Republicans a chance to win their vote in 2020. This is a historic opportunity for Republicans to regain the support of black Americans that liberal Republicans squandered in 1932 and 1936. But just how should you go about telling this powerful story to your brothers and sisters who are African Americans? If you read on, you will discover how to bring the truth to the black community.

The approach we explain has been repeatedly successful for numerous candidates, and the Donald Trump campaign, backed by a number of super PACs, validated it once again in 2016 and 2018. You and the groups you are active in can employ this approach on behalf of a local or statewide campaign, confident that it will be successful. A large percentage of black Americans are the natural allies of conservative Republicans, and it's time they join us under the Republican banner. The following detailed information provides an outline of what you need to know to share the truth and be successful in your area.

As was noted earlier, several super PACs cannot win 20 percent or even 25 percent of the black vote for Donald Trump by themselves. The Republican Party, its candidates at all levels, and public policy allies who support the right to life and the Second Amendment, as well as groups committed to lower taxes and strong economic growth, must do their part as well. These groups and individuals must run both social media and radio ad campaigns directed to black voters.

In addition, you and the organizations and candidates you support must reach out to and meet with voters in the black community (church groups, civic groups, veterans' groups, etc.). By doing so you will begin building a bond of trust with black Americans. This effort also will give you an opportunity to distribute literature directly to black Americans. The idea is to meet black Americans where they live and work, in barbershops and beauty shops, in their churches, and in their neighborhoods, going door to door and meeting with black voters and hearing their views.

In reality, the Trump campaign, the Republican National Committee (RNC), state Republican parties, U.S. Senate candidates, U.S. House of Representatives candidates, candidates for governor, and conservative issue groups (National Rifle Association, National Right to Life Committee, etc.) are the only entities with the resources to buy eight weeks of radio ads on urban contemporary radio to reach black voters age 35 and older. Your local organization probably can't do that, but the RNC and your state Republican Party can. What kinds of radio ads should they run? The ads should be high contrast. In other words, the ads must show the dramatic difference on issues of importance to the black community between the policies of conservative Republicans and those of radical Democrats.

Testing has shown that all radio ad campaigns should start with the pro-life issue, which has proved to be the gateway issue for reaching black voters.[452] This is even more imperative with today's Democrats embracing third-trimester abortions, selling body parts, and even advocating the killing of babies after they are born.[453] If the state GOP and statewide candidates run eight weeks of ads, for maximum effectiveness they should start with four issues, in this order:

1. The right to life
2. School choice
3. Jobs
4. A secure border

Even state legislative candidates and other candidates for local office can have a big impact with black voters by running four weeks of radio ads on black urban contemporary stations, placing several spots in rotation. But for a state legislative race, it is crucially important for conservative Republican candidates to go directly into the black community. This is the primary way a local candidate can make major inroads into the black vote. There, in the black community, he should meet with black pastors and black civic leaders. Such contacts will lead to opportunities to speak before black audiences.

If a candidate or a local GOP organization can run ads for only four weeks, it should limit its topics to the right to life, school choice, and jobs in that order. However, a word of caution is due. Utilizing high-contrast radio ads has been proved successful, but simply hiring a black conservative to reach out to the black community in your area will have little impact unless he has a plan and a budget to actually reach black voters. Conversely, funds spent on reaching black voters in person in the black community and on radio ads will be money well spent.

The Republican National Committee can help the party, candidates, and issues groups at every level by conducting a specially designed survey of black voters only, identifying those who are open to voting for Donald Trump in 2020. Such a survey will develop a demographic profile of the black people who voted for Trump in 2016, those who self-identify as conservative (about one-third), the 41 percent who approve of the president's job performance,[454] those who believe that they will be wealthier at the end of the Trump term, and those who didn't vote for Trump in 2016 but are open to voting for him in 2020. Once that profile is developed, it can be used to identify black voters who should be contacted by the official Trump organization and other groups supporting his reelection.

As was noted in the book, the 2016 Trump campaign had success using targeted digital advertising to reach black voters. One ad told black voters about Hillary Clinton's "super predator" comments: *"They are often the kinds of kids that are called 'super-predators.' No conscience, no empathy, we can talk about why they ended up that way, but first we have to bring them to heel."*[455] This ad caused black voters who strongly distrust the Republican Party yet have much in common with it to simply not vote for Clinton. Eventually, those black voters will become Republican voters. Online digital ads should target black voters on a number of issues that contrast the positions of Donald Trump on issues such as abortion, school choice, and energy with those of the Democratic candidate, who is sure to take a position with which a majority of black voters disagree. Such ads will bleed black support from Democrats and increase black support for the president.

The Trump campaign also can use special tools available through Facebook to identify likely black supporters. Facebook's Custom Audiences and customer lists commercial data make it possible to identify black supporters who have liked and/or positively interacted with their Facebook platforms. Then, using Lookalike Audiences, it is possible to identify black voters who fit that profile. In addition, any candidate or interest group with 5,000 black Facebook supporters can contact others, using that profile information. In this way, black conservative groups with at least 5,000 black supporters can expand the Trump coalition. Then, using these tools, they can reach undecided black voters in swing states who have not yet boarded the Trump "train."

How can a county GOP leadership team reach black voters? These local GOP leaders and elected officials should offer to speak to black voters in their community, including at the meetings of the service and civic organizations to which they belong. These organizations are always looking for speakers, and so a telephone call usually will result in an opportunity to speak to these black American civic leaders. A draft engagement speech can be found immediately after this section. The speech should express the desire of the speaker to work with and support the black community on issues such as (1) the right to life, (2) school choice, (3) jobs, (4) individual wealth creation, (5) secure borders, (6) the Second Amendment, and (7) criminal justice reform. For example, the right to life project entails working with the local crisis pregnancy center. Why is Republican support for a crisis pregnancy center in a black area important? To the extent that a black congregation sends women to that crisis pregnancy center to get help, sends money to it, or sends up prayers, a wedge is driven between that congregation and the Democratic Party. Democrats don't save black babies; they support Planned Parenthood, which aborts black babies up to and including full term and then sells their body parts. The other projects similarly suggest deep engagement with the black community.

Some GOP organizations choose to approach black voters on issues for which there is little or no contrast between the GOP and the Democratic Party. This does not give black voters any reason to vote for a Republican candidate over a Democratic candidate. In contrast, when a local Republican or conservative organization offers free professional seminars at churches to help black Americans accumulate wealth, it is providing a service the Democrats would never consider offering. Democrats have zero interest in helping black Americans move into the middle class because that would only bring those voters closer to the Republican Party. When you consider that only 10 percent of black voters get help from professional financial planners compared with 40 percent of the general population, the demand is significant in the black community. Such expert advice will be greatly appreciated, and when those services are offered by qualified experts at no cost, a significant bridge can be built to the black community. When a black man has a quarter million dollars in the stock market, he soon becomes a Donald Trump Republican. When black Americans accumulate wealth, Democratic appeals to class warfare no longer work because that voter knows that soaking the rich means reducing the capital gains and dividends that fuel his retirement portfolio.

At one presentation I [Vernon] made to a conservative organization, a grassroots activist asked if a black speaker would be better to engage black audiences. As a white person, she was afraid that she might come across as saying she is the black folks' savior. I answered that unlike the godless Democratic Party, black folks know who the Savior is. In fact, before I was a party official or an elected official, I gave a speech to a black audience in which one person commented that it was a good speech, but since I had no official role in the Republican Party, he wanted to hear directly from GOP leaders. In that case, I lacked credibility not because I was the wrong color but because black voters want to hear directly from an official of the Republican Party.

To be successful, the Republican Party and its candidates must engage directly with black voters and go door to door in the black community to make the case why Donald Trump deserves their vote. The GOP hasn't asked black voters for their support for 60 years, and no one has ever gotten the order without asking for the sale.

One super PAC, Black Americans to Re-Elect the President, printed a *Make Black America Great Again* booklet as its door-to-door engagement tool. That booklet is reprinted in this section. The booklet has three sections. The first section rejects the notion that the president is a racist by noting that for decades, as a businessman, he was feted by Al Sharpton and Jesse Jackson, even receiving a medal at the same time as the late civil rights pioneer Rosa Parks. The only reason Trump is falsely charged as a racist now is that he ran as a Republican against Hillary Clinton and beat her. There is no evidence of Trump ever supporting the racist policies that the Democrats regularly support.

The second section of the booklet quotes Democratic racist utterances such as the one from the white Maryland state delegate who said that campaigning in the mostly black 69th richest county in the nation was *"campaigning in a N-word district."*[456] It also provides racist quotes by Bill and Hillary Clinton and Joe Biden and points out a study that shows that Democrats talk down to minorities whereas conservatives speak the same way to all audiences regardless of minority makeup. That shows what Democrats really think about black Americans.

The third section of the booklet highlights the five high-contrast issues mentioned before: life, school choice, jobs, borders, and guns. The sixth issue is criminal justice reform; it is the number one issue for black women under age 40 and the number two issue after health care for black women over 40. This issue is in the booklet because although many people talked about it, President Trump actually delivered on the First Step Act criminal justice reform.

Individuals involved in grassroots conservative leadership at the county level have experimented with distributing these booklets. They have found success going door to door, leaving them in black barbershops and beauty shops, and handing them out to those voting early, at gun shows, and on Election Day. The materials produced by GOP candidates and local leaders don't have to have the same content as these booklets but should feature high-contrast, high-impact contemporary issues that affect black voters today.

Republican Party officials, elected GOP officeholders, allied issue groups, and grassroots activists must run a triple-threat offense to get 20 percent or more of the black vote in the key swing states in 2020. The three avenues of attack are (1) engagement speeches and highly focused projects in black communities year-round, (2) retail door-to-door advocacy, and (3) eight weeks of hard-hitting, high-contrast radio ads that reach 50 percent of the black electorate in targeted markets each week.

Make no mistake, the 2020 presidential election campaign probably will be decided by black voters again. That's why it is important to have all hands on deck for this battle. Right now, efforts are under way by super PACs to maximize the air campaign over black radio stations in key swing states. And at this moment, at least one black conservative super PAC is initiating a ground game in black areas to surge the black vote for Donald Trump. If the GOP at the national, state, and local level also does its part, black voters will again provide the margin of victory for Donald Trump in 2020.

Sample Speech

I thank you for inviting me to speak about empowering black citizens to reach the American dream. If you recall, many people, not just black Americans, held great hope when the first black president was elected in 2008, but his administration simply replayed failed liberal policies of the past.

In fact, regulations were increased, killing jobs. In addition to there being fewer available jobs, immigration policies encouraged foreign workers to compete with black citizens for them. Schools continued to fail to educate black children and especially black boys. Instead of addressing these challenges, the past administration sought to put men in women's bathrooms. The Obama administration attacked the moral beliefs of many families of every color, black and white, by devaluing natural marriage and aggrandizing alternative couplings. This former administration relaxed or removed work requirements and time limits for able-bodied welfare recipients with no dependents, increasing the welfare rolls. Black wages fell, black wealth fell, and home ownership fell for black and white Americans alike.

As a result, many Americans believed that the country was headed in the wrong direction. Black babies were killed by abortion at a rate three times that of white babies. Welfare and food stamp dependency went up for blacks.

The Trump administration has reversed many of these failed policies and sent both the economy and job opportunities through the ceiling. Black unemployment is now 5.9 percent, the lowest in recorded history. Black workforce participation is up. Consumer confidence is much higher. Welfare and Medicaid enrollments are down, as is the number of food stamp recipients. The new administration is drilling for new energy sources and has approved the pipeline deal, creating jobs, lowering the cost of energy, stimulating economic growth, and putting Venezuela, Iran, and Russia at a disadvantage.

I have come today to ask for your help to continue the current upward mobility for black Americans.

The first issue is life.

Black babies matter, and we must reverse policies and practices that result in black babies being killed by abortion at three times the rate of white babies. In New York City, 60 percent of black babies die by abortion. I hope you will join with me in denouncing the racist views of Margaret Sanger and stop federal funding to the organization she created to exterminate black people: Planned Parenthood. There is a reason Margaret Sanger was popular with the KKK.

I want you to work with me to support crisis pregnancy ministries that help women choose life for their babies and help new mothers after their children are born.

Republicans want to save babies regardless of color. Democratic elected officials support policies that kill black babies up to a minute before they are born and then sell baby body parts. The next time Democrats ask for your vote, I hope you will ask them why they do not want your children.

The second issue is restoring the ladder to economic opportunity. Once upon a time, government-run schools provided the ladder of upward mobility to those who were poor, particularly those in urban ghettos. Those schools also taught both those born here and legal immigrants why America is exceptional and how to be an American as well as how to read, write, and add. Now, many public schools do not teach children how to read, write, or add. Nor do they teach American values of limited constitutional government, free markets, and individual freedom. Perhaps most scary, children are not taught that the foundation of our republic is that rights come from God, not man. Instead, these schools hand out condoms, preach hate for America, and trample on the values held by decent folk, both white and black.

I ask you to not sacrifice another son or daughter to failing government-run public schools but instead support school choice schools that will give your children and grandchildren a great education. The Republican Party supports choice schools that affirm, not attack, your values. The Democratic Party opposes home schooling, opposes charter schools, and tries to regulate them out of existence.

I ask you to work with me, school reform groups, and the local home school organizations to support high-quality choice schools for your community and, in lieu of that, encourage black families to join the home school movement. We can agree that good schools, graduating from high school, avoiding single parenthood, getting married and staying married, and getting a good job are the key to raising black household incomes.

At the college level, the Democrats have watered down college by suppressing differing views on campuses and offering meaningless degrees in things like gender and ethnic studies, leaving students unprepared to be successful in life.

Work with me to elect legislators who will require independent agencies to track employment prospects and salaries for each major at our publicly funded colleges and universities and use that data to reallocate funding from unsuccessful programs to successful alternatives outside the college system. This data also will help college-bound students choose STEM college majors and the high-paying STEM careers.

We need solid community college programs that teach trades such as HVAC, plumbing, electrical work, and auto mechanics, which equip graduates for the high-paying trades. These trades are facing huge shortages of new entrants and are saddled with an aging workforce. This is a great opportunity for our young people.

Additionally, help me promote and scale up programs such as Praxis (www.discoverpraxis.com), which uses the apprentice approach to put people as young as 17 into a nine-month apprenticeship program with a guaranteed job and no college debt.

The third issue I would like to discuss with you is jobs, taxes, regulation, and increasing the wealth of your family. If you recall, many people, including Republicans, hoped that President Obama would succeed, but after the soaring words of his campaign, he embraced policies that created higher taxes, higher spending, and more regulation, choking the private economy. We also saw immigration policies hostile to the black middle and working classes.

The result of these policies were declining statistics in every category for black Americans. Black home ownership started going down in 2006 and did not turn up slightly until the first year of the Trump administration. Democrats talk about creating good jobs, but what they have created is more government jobs, more bureaucrats messing in your business, and fewer high-paying manufacturing jobs. The last administration created ten government jobs for every manufacturing job; in contrast, the Trump administration has created ten high-paying jobs in manufacturing for every new government job.

Some apologists for the Democratic agenda argue that black unemployment started to fall before Trump came in and the continued decline of black unemployment is a continuation of the Obama trend. Nothing could be farther from the truth. There are two ways to reduce unemployment. One is to create no new net private sector jobs and cushion the blow by expanding welfare and Medicaid. This was the approach of the last administration. It reduced the number of people looking for work, thus lowering the unemployment rate on paper, and put more able-bodied men without dependents on welfare.

The other way to reduce unemployment is to create more jobs than there are people to fill them, and that is what the Trump administration has done. By growing the economy at twice the rate of the prior government, Trump has reduced black unemployment and the gap between white and black employment to the lowest levels in history.[457] At the same time, we have increased black workforce participation.

The Democrats say tax the rich as if the top 10 percent of income earners are not paying their fair share. The reality is that the top 1 percent pays 40 percent of income taxes, the top 10 percent pays 71 percent, and the bottom 47 percent pay no income taxes. The bottom 17 percent got money from you and me through the earned income tax credit. How is that fair?

Dr. Ben Carson in his prayer breakfast speech said that *"the most compassionate force in the universe is God and He has a plan. It's called a tithe, 10 percent. Now God did not say if you had a good crop you pay triple tithes and if you had a bad year you pay no tithes. So there is something inherently fair and compassionate about proportionality. You make a billion you pay $100 million You make $10 thousand, you pay $1,000."*

The truth is that the Democrats want to raise taxes on you because there are not enough rich people to pay for their programs. Apparently, Democrats are more compassionate than God. I don't believe that they are more loving and compassionate than God, and neither do you.

The Trump tax cuts unleashed the most productive people in this country to create more jobs than there are people to fill them, jobs for everyone. These policies have put more in your pocket and in the pockets of everyone you know. Yet in spite of all this progress toward ending the class envy policies of the past and greatly expanding the economy, wage increases, and wealth creation, we still have a lot of work to do. Two big problems facing many black earners are bad credit and lack of professional financial planning. In fact, whereas 40 percent of the general public gets professional financial planning assistance, only 10 percent of black families do.

So I want to work with you on these two issues. Work with me to get our youth exposed to credit counselors so that they can learn how to establish good credit and keep it so good that it will help them buy their first house. I also want to work with you on wealth creation to increase your financial nest egg by bringing in a financial planner to provide free workshops on how to grow rich slowly.

The next issue I'm concerned about, and I'm sure you are too, is the attack on the black middle class by unlimited illegal immigration, open borders, and sanctuary cities. Our children, yours and mine, are dreamers too. But the Democratic Party places the interests of illegal aliens over those of American citizens. They have to get more foreigners voting because Democrats can no longer get a majority of the votes of native-born Americans. That makes you expendable. They support noncitizens and illegals voting like the 95,000 illegals registered to vote in Texas.[458] They downplay the threat of the violent MS-13 gang, even warning these criminals to help them escape ICE arrest. Their new motto is *"no borders, no wall, no USA at all."*[459] I kid you not.

Are illegals going to vote in favor of your interests? I don't think so. Illegals are not just taking jobs that Americans "won't do"; they are also putting black contractors, black bricklayers, and other black firms out of business. Illegals affect other jobs Americans want. For example, as more non–English speakers need banking services, more Spanish-speaking tellers will be needed. Black Americans need not apply.

There is no doubt that public sector jobs, such as teachers and other local and state government jobs, built the black middle class. Requirements that these workers speak foreign languages are a dagger at the throat of the black middle class.

Should illegal aliens crowd out black college applicants because sanctuary colleges and universities are giving them admissions preference over U.S. citizens, including your children?

Work with me to make sure that only citizens vote in our elections, to secure the borders of the United States, to deport illegals who are committing crimes in our community or threatening our economic stability, and to stop public colleges and universities from giving admissions preferences to illegals over your children.

The fifth issue is the right of self-defense.

The Republican Party is committed to protecting your right to keep and bear arms. The Democratic Party is committed to disarming Americans either by confiscation or by making firearms and ammunition too expensive to buy.

If you believe as I do that although we have made great strides in race relations, we still have some ways to go, why would you want to give up your right to keep and bear arms?

History tells us that armed blacks in the South were able to defend themselves from the Klan and the night riders. When police in Louisiana sought illegally to stop black teens from protesting for civil rights, the Deacons for Defense and Justice, armed black men, arrived and started calmly loading shotguns. The police backed off and did not harass the protesters anymore. Citizens are armed. Subjects and slaves are disarmed. Work with me to:

- Eliminate gun-free zones that are havens for evildoers intent on murder and mayhem
- Create and expand Second Amendment ministries in more churches
- Enroll more youth in gun safety and marksmanship youth programs
- Repeal the last Jim Crow law on the books, the pistol permit from the sheriff, historically used to disarm blacks
- Ensure that every law-abiding citizen is armed and knows how to use those weapons both for personal safety and to deter tyranny

The sixth issue I would like to talk to you about is criminal justice reform. Folks have talked about doing criminal justice reform for years. For many of the people in this audience, criminal justice reform is your top issue.

But it was just talk until President Trump, working with a broad bipartisan coalition that included Republican senators, conservative groups, and Kim Kardashian West, delivered and signed the First Step Act into law. The president's son-in-law Jared Kushner worked on this issue day and night to make prison reform happen.

The First Step Act restores the ability of judges to make determinations on sentencing, ending the bad old days of mandatory minimum sentencing at the federal level. The First Step Act is getting many more nonviolent offenders out of jail sooner. It ends the practice of shackling pregnant prisoners. Finally, it funds programs to help train and place prior nonviolent offenders in jobs when they have paid their debt to society.

But as the act implies, this is only a first step. Real change must happen in our communities, not in Washington. So with that in mind, I ask you to work with me, the local Goodwill Industries, and other community programs to help former offenders find and keep jobs, get their driver's licenses back, and get access to housing and also support prison ministries with their many programs, such as the one that collects gifts for the children of inmates at Christmas.

Thank you for having me today and in advance for working with me. By saving black babies, educating children, creating more jobs and business opportunities, stopping the illegal invasion, arming all law-abiding citizens, and pushing forward criminal justice reform, together we can make America great again.

2020 Persuasion Brochure

Part 1:

HOW TRUMP TRIGGERED RACISTS IN THE DEMOCRAT PARTY

Donald Trump has been in the public eye for well over 30 years and was never once accused of being racist by anyone.

That is, until he decided to run for President of the United States in 2016.

But why? Well, the answer is simple:

He spoke directly to black Americans asking them to abandon the Democrat Party for the true party of freedom – the Republican Party.

That's a big "no-no" for all Jim Crow Democrats who understand that if they lose just 15% of the black vote, they'll never win an election again.

Just 15%!

So these Democrats did what they do best:

Bashed Trump – and all Republicans – as "*racists*", "*bigots*" and "*white nationalists*".

The irony is that the real home of racism is the Democrat Party.
Not convinced?

Here's proof from their own racist mouths...

Part 2:

MODERN DAY JIM CROW RACISTS: DEMOCRAT PARTY 2018

"CROOKED HILLARY"

"They [black youths] are often the kinds of kids that are called 'super-predators,'...No conscience, no empathy, we can talk about why they ended up that way, but first we have to bring them to heel."

– 1996 speech.

HOUSE MINORITY LEADER
NANCY PELOSI (D-CA)

"This was such a proud day for me because when my grandson blew out the candles on his cake, they said, 'did you make a wish?'...He said, 'I wish I had brown skin and brown eyes like Antonio.' So beautiful, so beautiful. The beauty is in the mix."

VICE PRESIDENT JOE BIDEN

CHAMPION GAFFE MAKER

"You got the first mainstream African American who is articulate and bright and clean.. I mean that's storybook, man!"

Referring to Barack Obama, 1/13/2007

"You cannot go to a 7-11 or a Dunkin' Donuts unless you have a slight Indian accent.. I'm not joking!"

C-SPAN, 2008

"SLICK WILLIE"
PRESIDENT CLINTON
"A few years ago, [Barack Obama] would have been getting us coffee."

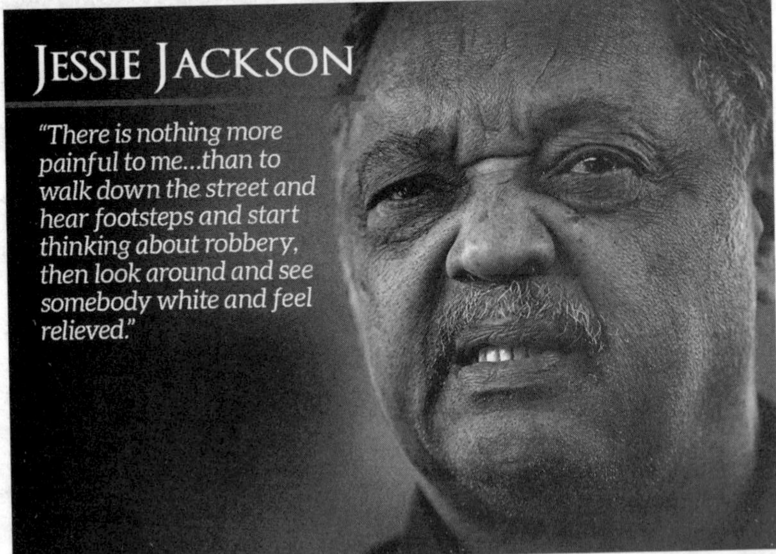
JESSIE JACKSON
"There is nothing more painful to me...than to walk down the street and hear footsteps and start thinking about robbery, then look around and see somebody white and feel relieved."

Part 3:

Exposing 5 Ways Racist Democrats are Keeping Blacks "Under Heel", and how Trump's Conservative Policies can **Set Them Free.**

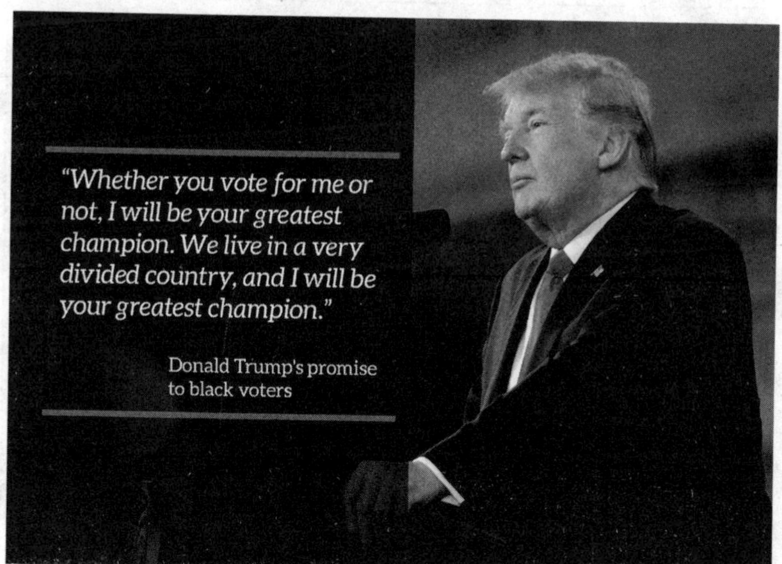

- **Trump:** Favors School Choice for all, and increasing vouchers and scholarships for black kids.

- **Jim Crow Democrats:** Support school choice for their kids, but deny to everyone else.

Once upon a time, government run schools provided upward mobility to those who were poor. Especially those in urban ghettoes.

Not only did these schools teach reading, writing, and math, they also taught them about American exceptionalism, limited Constitutional government, the free market, and that the foundation of the greatest country in the world is that rights come from God, not man.

Sadly, instead of teaching these things, schools today hand out condoms, preach hate about America, and trample on the values held by decent folk, both white and black.

Democrats are sacrificing our kids, especially in the inner cities, to enrich corrupt unions. No wonder during the 2016 election, Trump called school choice the "civil rights issue of our time," especially for African Americans.

> *African-American citizens have sacrificed so much for our nation. They fought and died in every war since the Revolution and from the pews and the picket lines, they've lifted up the conscience of our country in the long march for civil rights. Yet too many African-Americans have been left behind.*

And one of the greatest areas African Americans suffer is school choice.

This is all thanks to racists in the Democrat Party who deny blacks vouchers and school choice.

In fact, a majority of current Democrat Senators either went to private school, or have kids currently in private schools.

Senators like Robert Casey Jr (D-PA), Sheldon Whitehouse (D-RI), and Michael Bennet (D-CO).

Hypocrites!

The truth is that the Democrat Party opposes home schooling, charter schools, and anything that will lift black kids out of poverty.

The Republican Party and President Trump supports school choice, home schools, and your values.

- **Trump:** Supports empowering black Americans through free market policies.
- **Jim Crow Democrats:** Support flooding the job market with illegals.

Barack Obama won over 90% of the black vote, but left black voters worse off than they were before he was in office. Black income, home ownership, and employment rates fell more than any other racial group.

Yet, since President Trump took office, black American employment has risen by over 600,000 to near all-time highs, and black ownership is on the rebound.

That's spells doom for Jim Crow Democrats and explains why they're playing the race card.

- **Trump:** Supports life and hates the concept of abortion. Like all Republicans, he wants to save babies regardless of color.

- **Jim Crow Democrats:** Support killing black babies.

Democrats want everyone to know that they're "pro-choice." But what they don't like to talk about is how over 900 black babies are aborted every day!

That comes out to more than 19 million black babies killed since the 1973 Roe v. Wade decision.

Talk about genocide!

If that isn't bad enough, have you ever heard of Margaret Sanger? Sanger created what eventually became Planned Parenthood Federation of America – the group responsible for aborting millions of black babies.

Just look at what she thinks about black babies.

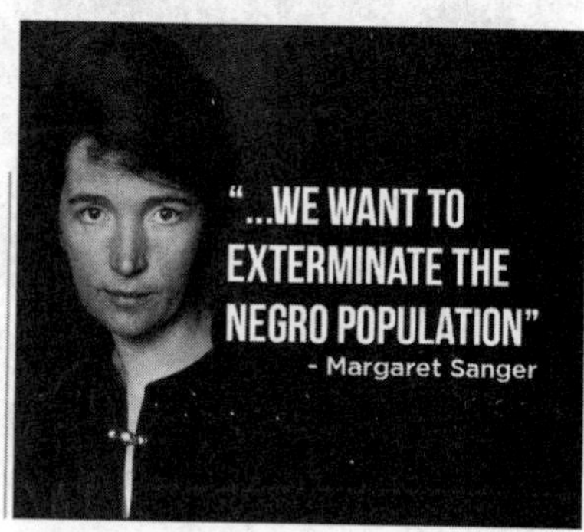

Or how about what **prominent Democrat** politicians think about her?

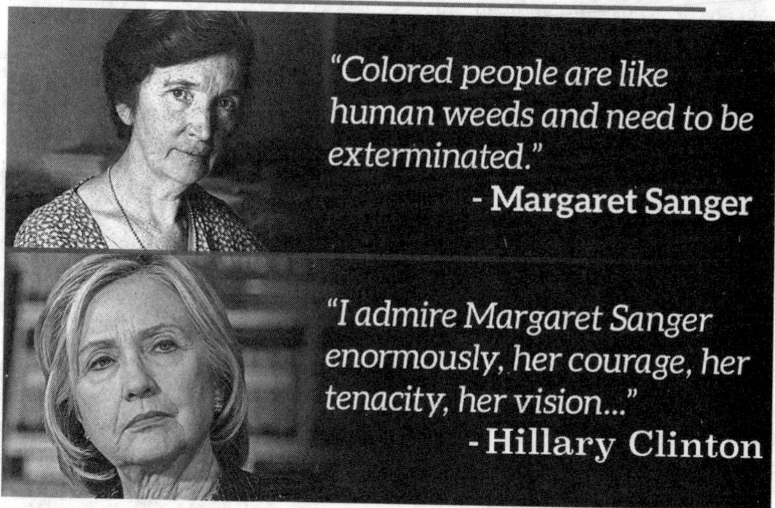

Or what **President Obama** thinks about her organization – Planned Parenthood.

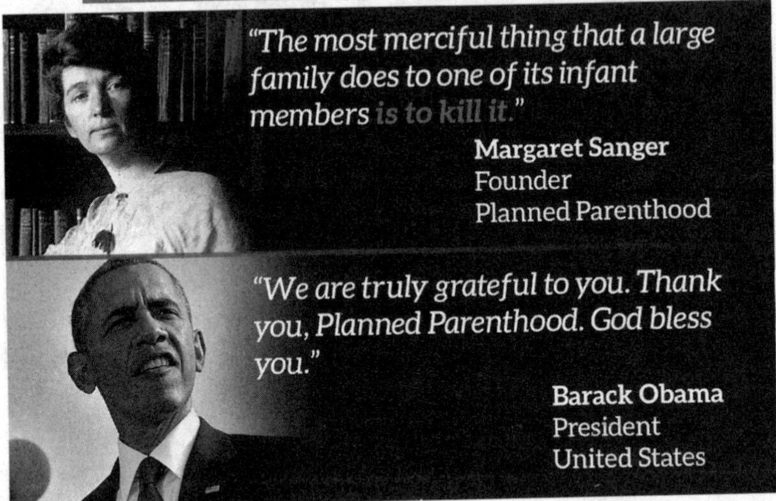

The next time a Democrat asks for your vote, **I hope you'll ask them why** he or she does not want your children.

Black children are dreamers too.

But the Democrat Party places the interests of illegal aliens over American citizens.

Heck, they even shut down the government for illegals.

Why are they doing this?

Simple: the Democrat Party knows they can no longer get a majority of the votes of native born Americans, so they must import foreigners.

That makes you expendable.

Their new motto is no borders, no wall, no USA at all!

And illegals aren't just taking the jobs that Americans "won't do." They are putting black contractors, black bricklayers, and other Americans out of business.

President Trump and the Republican Party want to make sure only citizens can vote in our elections. He wants to secure our borders, and deport all illegals who are committing crimes in our communities.

In short, he wants to put America and Americans first.

- **Trump and Republicans:** Support black's - and all Americans' - right to keep and bear arms.

- **Jim Crow Democrats:** Support disarming Americans by confiscation or by making guns and ammo too expensive to buy.

Citizens are Armed. Subjects and Slaves are Disarmed.

History tells us that armed blacks in the south were able to defend themselves from the Klan and the night riders.

When police in Louisiana sought to illegally stop black teens from protesting for civil rights, the Deacons for Defense and Justice, armed black men, arrived and started calmly loading shotguns.

The police backed off and did not harass the protesters any more.

Republicans and President Trump believe in:

✓ Eliminating gun free zones that are havens for evil doers intent on murder and mayhem.

✓ Creating and expanding 2nd amendment ministries in more churches, to enroll more youths in gun safety and marksmanship youth programs.

✓ Repealing the last Jim Crow law on the books - the pistol permit from the sheriff, historically used to disarm blacks.

✓ And ensuring that every law abiding citizen is armed and knows how to use those weapons both for personal safety and to deter tyranny.

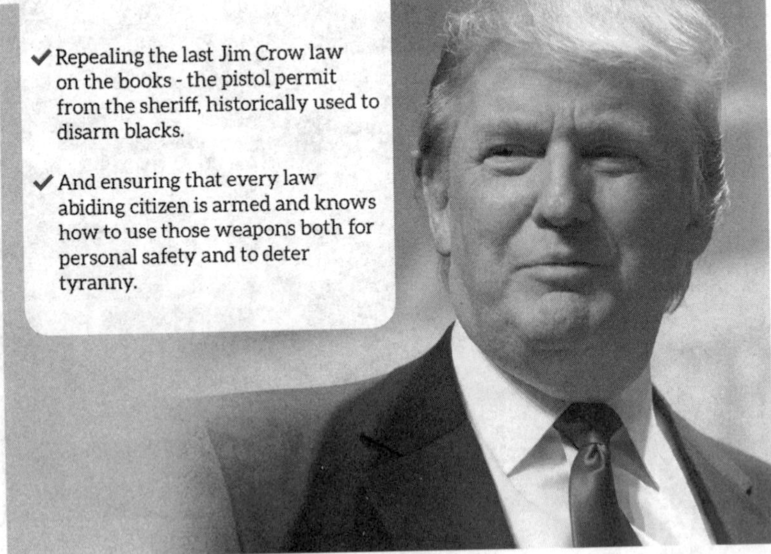

MAGA

I hope this little book has **opened your eyes** to how the Democrat Party has kept blacks under heel for generations in order to get their vote.

I hope and pray you'll support Black Americans for the President's Agenda as we support President Trump's efforts to:

- ✔ Save black babies
- ✔ Provide school choice for black kids
- ✔ Create more jobs for blacks to lift them out of poverty
- ✔ Stop the invasion of illegal aliens
- ✔ Arm all law abiding citizens so they can protect themselves

Not only will your support help make sure President Trump can Make America Great Again, you'll help **Make Black America Great Again**.

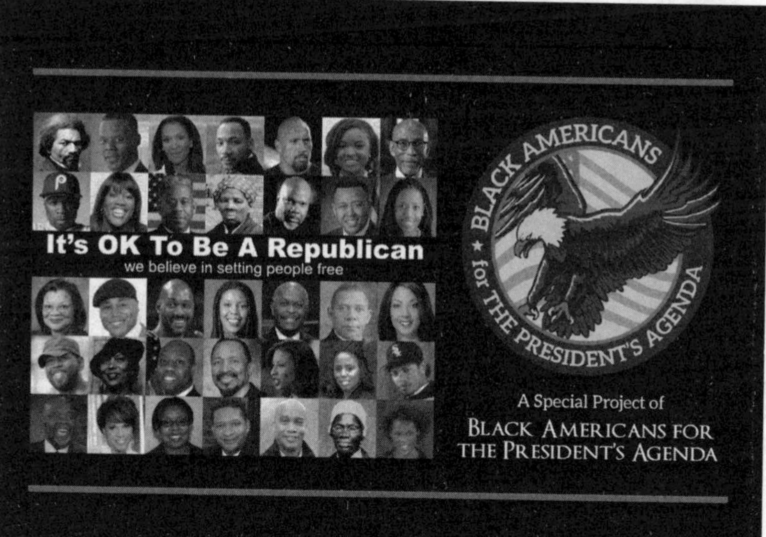

Note: Actual brochure is in full color. Copies of this and similar brochures are available in bulk quantities directly from Black Americans to Re-Elect the President, vrobinson679@gmail.com, 2713 Edinberg Drive, Winston-Salem, NC 27103.

ACKNOWLEDGMENTS

The authors wish to thank the many generous individuals who contributed directly to the publication of this book and also those who simply provided encouragement along the way. The first of these encouragers was Lee Edwards. In fact, Lee provided the impetus for writing this book when he was asked why a group called Young Americans for Freedom lent no support to the civil rights movement of the 1960s. His answer to that question and his answers to subsequent questions played a huge role in making this book a reality. Thanks, Lee. Early on, the kind comments, good advice, and encouragement given by Christopher Long, president of the Philadelphia Society, kept the project moving forward. In fact, almost everywhere we turned, we received help and encouragement, including from Intercollegiate Studies Institute and from conservative friends such as Allan Ryskind and Jim Roberts. Thank you one and all.

Although the idea of writing a book is exciting, the actual writing and research can be challenging. Kathi Eberle provided not only encouragement but also a special kind of proofreading that only wives can give. That special proofreading included critiques, insights, and plain comments that this paragraph is "unintelligible" or "what does this sentence mean?" Kathi's encouragement and commonsense advice certainly made this book much more readable and understandable. Thank you, Kathi. Also, a special thanks to "superproofreader" John Livingstone, who took time out of his very busy life to go over this book with an eagle eye. A special thank you to Michael Garner, who read the manuscript with an eye to historical accuracy and to the effective communication of ideas. Michael, your advice and comments were invaluable.

We also want to thank Stella Pecot Robinson, a truly courageous American who risked her life on behalf of civil rights for black Americans, especially for her children, who were yet unborn. Stella, you are an inspiration to generations of Americans, black and white, who fought for and made a better place for Americans of all races. Stella provided insight into the incredible obstacles placed in the way of black Americans in the South, especially in the 1930s and 1940s. You have never stopped being a pioneer in fighting for the basic constitutional rights of black American citizens. You are a true American hero.

Of course, we also want to thank the hardworking and perseverant folks at Shirley & Banister Public Affairs. Diana, you jumped right into the fray as our literary agent, and Craig, you continually assured us that we would find the right publisher, and we did, thanks to the tireless efforts of Kevin McVicker, who expertly led us through the web that is book publishing and marketing. Thanks also to Mitchell Shirley for his efforts to market this book. The work of everyone at Shirley & Banister is greatly appreciated.

Then there are the hardworking, smart, and kind people at Humanix Books, especially Mary Glenn and her team, who turned a manuscript into the book you are reading. The folks at Humanix could not have been nicer, smarter, or more encouraging. They are terrific.

Finally, we wish to acknowledge that any mistakes, errors, or misquotes are solely the responsibility of the authors. Pro Gloria Dei.

Notes

INTRODUCTION

1. The Perpetuation of Our Political Institutions: Abraham Lincoln's Address to the Young Men's Lyceum of Springfield, Illinois, 27 January 1838, Collected Works of Abraham Lincoln, Sangamon Journal, http://www.abrahamlincolnonline.org/lincoln/speeches/lyceum.htm.
2. President Lincoln delivered the 272-word Gettysburg Address on November 19, 1863 on the battlefield near Gettysburg, Pennsylvania.
3. David Krayden, "Eric Holder: 'When Did You Think America Was Great?'," *Daily Caller*, March 29, 2019, https://dailycaller.com/2019/03/29/eric-holder-america-never-great-maga/.
4. Joshua Charles, *Liberty's Secrets: The Lost Wisdom of America's Founders* (Washington, D.C.: WND Books, 2015), 33.
5. Rush Limbaugh, "My Conversation with Ben Shapiro," *The Limbaugh Letter*, April 2019, 8.
6. "Population Estimates, July 1, 2018, (V2018)," United States Census Bureau, https://www.census.gov/quickfacts/pa; "Voting and Registration in the Election of November 2016," United States Census Bureau, https://www.census.gov/data/tables/time-series/demo/voting-and-registration/p20-580.html. Population of Pennsylvania 12,807,060, 11.9% black Americans, 74.5% of black population registered to vote, 59.4% black voting participation in 2016 election, 21% vote for Trump by black Pennsylvania voters = 141,631 black votes for Donald Trump. "Pennsylvania Statewide," Axiom Strategies, www.RemingtonResearchGroup.com. Survey conducted November 1 through November 2, 2016, 21% of black voters indicated they intended to vote for Donald Trump.
7. Kayla Fontenot, Jessica Semega, and Melissa Kollar, "Income and Poverty in the United States: 2017," U.S. Census Bureau publication, September 2018, 12, table 3.
8. Theodore R. Johnson, "What Nixon Can Teach the GOP About Courting Black Voters," *Politico*, August 15, 2015, https://www.politico.com/magazine/story/2015/08/what-nixon-can-teach-the-gop-about-courting-black-voters-121392.

9. Thomas B. Edsall, "Permanent Democratic Majority: New Study Says Yes," *Huffington Post*, December 6, 2017, https://www.huffpost.com/entry/pemanent-democratic-major_n_186257.

CHAPTER 1, DONALD TRUMP'S PARTY

10. Terry Jones, "Deregulation Nation: President Trump Cuts Regulations at Record Rate," *Investor's Business Daily*, August 14, 2018, https://www.investors.com/politics/commentary/deregulation-nation-president-trump-cuts-regulations-at-record-rate/.
11. Philip Klein, "Trump Declares Obamacare Is 'Over' as He Signs Individual Mandate Repeal into Law," *Washington Examiner*, December 22, 2017, https://www.washingtonexaminer.com/trump-declares-obamacare-is-over-as-he-signs-individual-mandate-repeal-into-law.
12. Tommy Binion, "The Incredible Trump Agenda—What Most Americans Don't Know About the War the President Has Waged," *Heritage Foundation*, March 5, 2018, https://www.heritage.org/conservatism/commentary/the-incredible-trump-agenda-what-most-americans-dont-know-about-the-war-the.
13. Kay Coles James speech given at the McLean Ladies Republican Club on December 20, 2018, at the River Bend Country Club, and heard by Bruce Eberle and his wife, Kathi.
14. Stephen Dinan and David Sherfinski, "Trump's Rousing CPAC Speech Cements New Direction in the Conservative Movement," *Washington Times*, March 3, 2019, https://www.washingtontimes.com/news/2019/mar/3/donald-trump-steers-cpac-message-in-new-direction/.
15. Terry Jones, "Deregulation Nation: President Trump Cuts Regulations at Record Rate," *Investor's Business Daily*, August 14, 2018, https://www.investors.com/politics/commentary/deregulation-nation-president-trump-cuts-regulations-at-record-rate/.
16. Julie Allen, "NATO Members Increase Defence Spending by $100 Billion after Donald Trump Called Them 'Delinquents,'" *Telegraph*, January 27, 2019, https://www.telegraph.co.uk/news/2019/01/27/nato-members-increase-defence-spending-100-billion-donald-trump/.
17. President Trump speech to the Conservative Political Action Conference (CPAC) on March 2, 2019.
18. Jill Colvin, "Donald Trump a 'Blue-Collar Billionaire' with a Lot of Money," *AP – Business Insider*, July 18, 2016, https://www.businessinsider.com/ap-donald-trump-a-blue-collar-billionaire-with-a-lot-of-money-2016-7.
19. U.S. Department of Defense, *FY 2019 Defense Budget*, https://dod.defense.gov/News/SpecialReports/Budget2019.aspx.
20. Chuck DeVore, "312,000 Jobs Added in December, Manufacturing Growing 714% Faster under Trump than Obama," *Forbes*, January 4, 2019, https://www.forbes.com/sites/chuckdevore/2019/01/04/312000-jobs-added-in-december-manufacturing-growing-714-faster-under-trump-than-obama/#70dd99935b50.
21. *Ibid.*

22. Chuck DeVore, "The Trump Manufacturing Jobs Boom: 10 Times Obama's over 21 Months," *Forbes*, October 16, 2018, https://www.forbes.com/sites/chuckdevore/2018/10/16/the-trump-manufacturing-jobs-boom-10-times-obamas-over-21-months/#7b269f645850.
23. Andrea Riquier, "Manufacturing Jobs Growing at Fastest Rate in 23 Years," *Barron's Market Watch*, August 3, 2018, https://www.marketwatch.com/story/heres-why-manufacturing-jobs-growth-has-been-so-strong-2018-08-03.
24. Chuck DeVore, "Manufacturers Added 6 Times More Jobs under Trump Than under Obama's Last 2 Years," *Forbes*, February 1, 2019, https://www.forbes.com/sites/chuckdevore/2019/02/01/manufacturers-added-6-times-more-jobs-under-trump-than-under-obamas-last-2-years/#1a4689445635.
25. Paul R. La Monica, "Black Unemployment Rate Hits a Record Low," *CNN Business*, June 1, 2018, https://money.cnn.com/2018/06/01/news/economy/black-unemployment-rate-record-low/index.html.
26. Gabrielle Pickard-Whitehead, "Wow! American Small Business Ownership Up 400% in a Year, Survey Reveals," Small Business Trends, August 9, 2018, https://smallbiztrends.com/2018/08/african-american-small-business-statistics-2018.html; Andrea Riquier, "Manufacturing Jobs Growing at Fastest Rate in 23 Years," *Barron's Market Watch*, August 3, 2018, https://www.marketwatch.com/story/heres-why-manufacturing-jobs-growth-has-been-so-strong-2018-08-03.
27. Katherine Rodriguez, "5.8 Million Individuals Drop Off Food Stamps under Trump," *Breitbart*, June 19, 2019, https://www.breitbart.com/economy/2019/06/19/million-individuals-drop-off-food-stamps-under-trump/.
28. Alex Williams, "Franklin Graham: Donald Trump Has Defended Christianity More Than Any President in My Lifetime," Premier Christian Radio, January 23, 2018, https://www.premierchristianradio.com/News/World/Franklin-Graham-Donald-Trump-has-defended-Christianity-more-than-any-president-in-my-lifetime.
29. Donald Trump won 21% of the black vote in Pennsylvania, the highest black support for a Republican candidate for president since Richard Nixon in 1960 when he won 32% of the black vote. See endnote 6.
30. "A majority of voters give Trump thumbs-up again, while Trudeau lags behind at 43% job approval; Trump's support with his base has increased drastically; Nearly half of Hispanics approve of Trump." Zogby Analytics, August 15, 2019.
31. Expressed by Hume at a meeting of the board of Trustees of Youth for Tomorrow in 2018.
32. David Brody and Scott Lamb, *The Faith of Donald J. Trump: A Spiritual Biography* (New York: HarperCollins Publishers, 2018).
33. Victor Davis Hanson, *The Case for Trump* (New York: Basic Books, 2019), 18.

34. Daniel Halper, "Jesse Jackson Once Sang Donald Trump's Praises," *New York Post*, August 31, 2016, https://nypost.com/2016/08/31/jesse-jackson-once-sang-donald-trumps-praises/.

CHAPTER 2, CONSERVATIVE FAILURE

35. Alvin Felzenberg, "How William F. Buckley, Jr., Changed His Mind on Civil Rights," *Politico*, May 13, 2017, https://www.politico.com/magazine/story/2017/05/13/william-f-buckley-civil-rights-215129.
36. William Voegeli, "Civil Rights and the Conservative Movement," *Claremont Institute CRB* VIII, no. 3 (Summer 2008), https://www.claremont.org/crb/article/civil-rights-and-the-conservative-movement/.
37. *Ibid.*
38. Alvin Felzenberg, "How William F. Buckley, Jr., Changed His Mind on Civil Rights," *Politico*, May 13, 2017, https://www.politico.com/magazine/story/2017/05/13/william-f-buckley-civil-rights-215129.
39. William Voegeli, "Civil Rights and the Conservative Movement," *Claremont Institute CRB* VIII, no. 3 (Summer 2008), https://www.claremont.org/crb/article/civil-rights-and-the-conservative-movement/.
40. *Ibid.*
41. *Ibid.*
42. Bruce heard this story from a senior conservative leader (at a lunch on July 10, 2018) who knew Buckley, and then confirmed its authenticity with Alan Ryskind, former editor of Human Events who had heard the same story. However Ryskind's recollection was that it wasn't a group of young conservatives, but just one individual who had this exchange with Buckley. Nevertheless, the question to Buckley and the response from him were consistent with the story Bruce heard.
43. Donald T. Critchlow, "Conservatism and Civil Rights," *Claremont University CRB* VIII, no. 4 (Fall 2008), accessed October 9, 2018, https://www.claremont.org/crb/article/conservatism-and-civil-rights/.
44. "The drafting of the bill was performed early in 1870 by Senator Charles Sumner, a dominant Radical Republican in the Senate, with the assistance of John Mercer Langston, a prominent African American who established the law department at Howard University. The bill was proposed by Senator Sumner and co-sponsored by Representative Benjamin F. Butler, both Republicans from Massachusetts, in the 41st Congress of the United States in 1870. Congress removed the coverage of public schools that Sumner had included. The act was passed by the 43rd Congress in February 1875 as a memorial to honor Sumner, who had just died. It was signed into law by U.S. President Ulysses S. Grant on March 1, 1875." "Civil Rights Act of 1875," Wikipedia, https://en.wikipedia.org/wiki/Civil_Rights_Act_of_1875.
45. Donald T. Critchlow, "Conservatism and Civil Rights," *Claremont University CRB* VIII, no. 4 (Fall 2008), accessed October 9, 2018, https://www.claremont.org/crb/article/conservatism-and-civil-rights/.

46. Russell Kirk and James McClellan, *The Political Principles of Robert A. Taft* (New York: Fleet Press, 1967), 76.
47. Donald T. Critchlow, "Conservatism and Civil Rights," *Claremont University CRB* VIII, no. 4 (Fall 2008), accessed October 9, 2018, https://www.claremont.org/crb/article/conservatism-and-civil-rights/.
48. Crystal Wright, "How Liberal Policies Destroyed Black Families," *Daily Signal*, March 29, 2016, https://www.dailysignal.com/2016/03/29/how-liberal-policies-destroyed-black-families/.
49. While the search for such stories or events by the authors was admittedly not exhaustive, we simply did not find any speeches or articles that strongly supported the civil rights of black Americans during this period.
50. Lee Edwards, *Just Right: A Life in Pursuit of Liberty* (Wilmington: ISI Books, 2017), 29.
51. Arnold L. Steinberg, *Whiplash!: From JFK to Donald Trump, a Political Odyssey* (Ottawa: Jameson Books, Inc., 2017), 109.
52. This exchange is taken from a transcript of an Interview of Lee Edwards by Bruce Eberle at the Heritage Foundation on July 10, 2018.
53. Associated Press, "Trump to Black Voters: What Do You Have to Lose?," YouTube video, August 19, 2016, https://www.youtube.com/watch?v=t-jasg-_E5M.
54. "Population Estimates, July 1, 2018, (V2018)," United States Census Bureau, https://www.census.gov/quickfacts/pa; "Voting and Registration in the Election of November 2016," United States Census Bureau, https://www.census.gov/data/tables/time-series/demo/voting-and-registration/p20-580.html. Population of Pennsylvania 12,807,060, 11.9% black Americans, 74.5% of black population registered to vote, 59.4% black voting participation in 2016 election, 21% vote for Trump by black Pennsylvania voters = 141,631 black votes for Donald Trump. "Pennsylvania Statewide," Axiom Strategies, www.RemingtonResearchGroup.com. Survey conducted November 1 through November 2, 2016, 21% of black voters indicated they intended to vote for Donald Trump.
55. "A majority of voters give Trump thumbs-up again, while Trudeau lags behind at 43% job approval; Trump's support with his base has increased drastically; Nearly half of Hispanics approve of Trump." Zogby Analytics, August 15, 2019, https://zogbyanalytics.com/news/896-a-majority-of-voters-give-trump-thumbs-up-again-while-trudeau-lags-behind-at-43-job-approval-trump-s-support-with-his-base-has-increased-drastically-nearly-half-of-hispanics-approve-of-trump.

CHAPTER 3, AGAIN IN 2020?

56. Nancy J. Weiss, *Farewell to the Party of Lincoln* (Princeton: Princeton University Press, 1983), 30.
57. *Ibid.*, 13.
58. David W. Southern, *The Progressive Era and Race: Reaction and Reform, 1900-1917* (Wheeling: Harlan Davidson, Inc., 2005), 24.

59. John M. Sears, "Black Americans and the New Deal," *Society for Higher Education Journal*, November 1976, 91.
60. Charles H. Martin, "Negro Leaders, the Republican Party, and the Election of 1932," *Phylon (1960-)* 32, no. 1 (1971): 87.
61. George F. Garcia, "Herbert Hoover and the Issue of Race" *Annals of Iowa*, 1979, 505-507.
62. Harvard Sitkoff, *A New Deal for Blacks: The Emergence of Civil Rights as a National Issue: The Depression Decade* (New York: Oxford University Press, 1978), 71.
63. *Ibid.*
64. Nancy J. Weiss, *Farewell to the Party of Lincoln* (Princeton: Princeton University Press, 1983), 185.
65. *Ibid.*
66. *Ibid.*, 185-186.
67. *Ibid.*, 180.
68. Republican National Committee Press Release, August 3, 1936, box P3, Claude A. Barnett papers, Chicago Historical Society, Chicago.
69. Paul W. Ward, "Wooing the Negro Vote," *Nation*, August 1, 1936.
70. Nancy J. Weiss, *Farewell to the Party of Lincoln* (Princeton: Princeton University Press, 1983), 186-193.
71. "The New Deal was a series of programs and projects instituted during the Great Depression by President Franklin D. Roosevelt that aimed to restore prosperity to Americans." "New Deal," History, June 6, 2019, https://www.history.com/topics/great-depression/new-deal. It was largely unsuccessful.
72. Arthur M. Schlesinger, Jr., *The Politics of Upheaval* (Boston: Houghton Mifflin, 1960), 430.
73. Nancy J. Weiss, *Farewell to the Party of Lincoln* (Princeton: Princeton University Press, 1983), 20.
74. S. Mintz and S. McNeil (2018), "African Americans and the New Deal," *Digital History* ID 3447, http://www.digitalhistory.uh.edu/disp_textbook_print.cfm?smtid=2&psid=3447.
75. Daphney Daniel, "How Blacks Became Blue: The 1936 African American Voting Shift from the Party of Lincoln to the New Deal Coalition" (Pell Scholars and Senior Theses, Salve Regina University, 2012), paper 77, http://digitalcommons.salve.edu/pell_theses.
76. *Ibid.*
77. David Robertson, *Sly and Able: A Political Biography of James F. Byrnes* (New York: W.W. Norton & Company, 1994), 92.
78. Virginia Van Der Veer, "Hugo Black and the K.K.K.," *American Heritage* 19, no. 3 (April 1968), https://www.americanheritage.com/content/hugo-black-and-kkk.
79. David W. Southern, *The Progressive Era and Race: Reaction and Reform, 1900-1917* (Wheeling: Harlan Davidson, Inc., 2005), 24.
80. Phillip Bump, "The Fix: When Did Black Americans Start Voting So Heavily Democratic," *Washington Post*, July 7, 2015, https://

www.washingtonpost.com/news/the-fix/wp/2015/07/07/when-did-black-americans-start-voting-so-heavily-democratic/?noredirect=on&utm_term=.36e7971fc56f.

81. Brooks Johnson. Trump's Numbers October 2019 Update, FActCheck.Org, October 11, 2019; https://www.factcheck.org/2019/10/trumps-numbers-october-2019-update/
82. Phillip Bump, "The Fix: When Did Black Americans Start Voting So Heavily Democratic," *Washington Post*, July 7, 2015, https://www.washingtonpost.com/news/the-fix/wp/2015/07/07/when-did-black-americans-start-voting-so-heavily-democratic/?noredirect=on&utm_term=.36e7971fc56f.

CHAPTER 4, A LIBERAL NIGHTMARE

83. David W. Southern, *The Progressive Era and Race: Reaction and Reform, 1900-1917* (Wheeling: Harlan Davidson, Inc., 2005), 47.
84. *Ibid.*
85. *Ibid.*
86. Olivia B. Waxman, "How the KKK's Influence Spread in Northern States," *Time*, October 24, 2017, http://time.com/4990253/kkk-white-nationalists-history/.
87. "Ku Klux Klan: A History of Racism," Southern Poverty Law Center, March 1, 2011, https://www.splcenter.org/20110228/ku-klux-klan-history-racism#klan-ruled-oregon.
88. David Brennan, "Finding Parents' MAGA Hats Will One Day Be Equivalent of Discovering Their 'Ku Klux Klan Hood,' Says Professor," *Newsweek*, February 18, 2019, https://www.newsweek.com/donald-trump-maga-hats-matt-sears-ku-klux-klan-racism-1334442.
89. History Extra, "When the Ku Klux Klan Was a Mass Movement," *BBC History Magazine*, September 2018, https://www.historyextra.com/period/20th-century/ku-klux-klan-mass-movement-organisation-secret-society-rise-american-south-1920s/.
90. "Ku Klux Klan Members in United States Politics," Wikipedia, https://en.wikipedia.org/wiki/Ku_Klux_Klan_members_in_United_States_politics.
91. Dinesh D'Souza, *The Big Lie: Exposing the Nazi Roots of the American Left* (Washington, D.C.: Regnery Publishing, Inc., 2017), 120.
92. The far left, violent ANTIFA group proclaims itself to be an anti-Fascist organization, but it reality it has many similarities to the violent "Black Shirts" organized by Benito Mussolini, the lifelong socialist and founder of the Fascist Party. Mussolini was a leftist praised by Vladimir Lenin for his formation of the Fascist Party. Like the Black Shirts, ANTIFA disrupts speeches and events featuring individuals who oppose socialism and advocate for individual freedom and free speech.
93. Peter Hermann, Keith L. Alexander, and Michael E. Miller, "Protesters Who Destroyed Property on Inauguration Day Were Part of Well-Organized Group," *Washington Post*, January 21, 2017, https://

www.washingtonpost.com/local/public-safety/protesters-who-destroyed-property-on-inauguration-day-part-of-well-organized-group/2017/01/21/096678c8-dfeb-11e6-ad42-f3375f271c9c_story.html?utm_term=.b3aa5f8519f8.

94. "Ku Klux Klan Members in United States Politics: Robert Byrd," Wikipedia, https://en.wikipedia.org/wiki/Ku_Klux_Klan_members_in_United_States_politics.
95. Benjy Sarlin, "Antifa Violence Is Ethical? This Author Explains Why," *NBC News*, August 20, 2017, https://www.nbcnews.com/politics/white-house/antifa-violence-ethical-author-explains-why-n796106.
96. Jennifer Rubin, "Trump's Era of Hate," *Washington Post*, November 14, 2018, https://www.washingtonpost.com/news/opinions/wp/2018/11/14/trumps-era-of-hate/?utm_term=.07c90efe75cc.
97. Dinesh D'Souza, *The Big Lie: Exposing the Nazi Roots of the American Left* (Washington, D.C.: Regnery Publishing, Inc., 2017), 5.
98. *Ibid*., 25.
99. "In 1838 and 1839, as part of Andrew Jackson's Indian removal policy, the Cherokee nation was forced to give up its lands east of the Mississippi River and to migrate to an area in present-day Oklahoma. The Cherokee people called this journey the "Trail of Tears," because of its devastating effects. The migrants faced hunger, disease, and exhaustion on the forced march. Over 4,000 out of 15,000 of the Cherokees died." "The Trail of Tears," PBS, https://www.pbs.org/wgbh/aia/part4/4h1567.html.
100. Abraham Lincoln named three prominent Northern Democrats who supported slavery: President Franklin Pierce (NH), President James Buchanan (PA), and Democrat presidential candidate Stephen Douglas (IL). Dinesh D'Souza, "D'Souza Proves Northern Democrats Supported Slavery Too," video, May 15, 2018, https://www.dineshdsouza.com/news/northern-democrats-supported-slavery/.
101. Calvin R. Evans, "Legacy: John F. Kennedy—His Real Civil Rights Record," *Black Star News*, November 22, 2013, http://www.blackstarnews.com/us-politics/justice/legacy-john-f-kennedy-his-real-civil-rights-record.html.
102. Tiffany Jones Miller, "Progressivism, Race, and the Training Wheels of Freedom," *National Review*, November 14, 2011, 37.
103. C. Vann Woodward, *The Strange Career of Jim Crow* (New York: Oxford University Press, 2002), 85.
104. David W. Southern, *The Progressive Era and Race: Reaction and Reform, 1900-1917* (Wheeling: Harlan Davidson, Inc., 2005), 2-3.
105. C. Vann Woodword, *Origins of the New South 1877-1913* (Baton Rouge: Louisiana State University Press, 1951, 1971), 91.
106. *Ibid.*
107. C. Vann Woodword, *Origins of the New South 1877-1913* (Baton Rouge: Louisiana State University Press, 1951, 1971), 371.
108. David W. Southern, *The Progressive Era and Race: Reaction and Reform, 1900-1917* (Wheeling: Harlan Davidson, Inc., 2005), 46-47.

109. *Ibid.*, 48.
110. Benjamin G. Rader, *The Academic Mind and Reform: The Influence of Richard T. Ely in American Life* (Lexington: University of Kentucky Press, 1966), 235.
111. David W. Southern, *The Progressive Era and Race: Reaction and Reform, 1900-1917* (Wheeling: Harlan Davidson, Inc., 2005), 48.
112. Michael Guillen, "Physicist: Don't Fall for the Argument about 'Settled Science'," *Fox News Channel*, January 21, 2019, https://www.foxnews.com/opinion/physicist-dont-fall-for-the-argument-about-settled-science.
113. David W. Southern, *The Progressive Era and Race: Reaction and Reform, 1900-1917* (Wheeling: Harlan Davidson, Inc., 2005), 49.
114. Jessica Chasmar, "Joe Biden: Dregs of Society Support Donald Trump," *Washington Times*, September 17, 2018, https://www.washingtontimes.com/news/2018/sep/17/joe-biden-dregs-society-have-ally-donald-trump/.
115. Joshua Charles, *Liberty's Secrets: The Lost Wisdom of America's Founders* (Washington, D.C.: WND Books, 2015), 85.
116. Benjamin Rush, "Of the Mode of Education Proper in a Republic," Selected Writings of Benjamin Rush, Volume 1, Chapter 18, Document 30, http:press-pubs.uchicago.edu/founders/documents/v1ch18s30.html.
117. Joshua Charles, *Liberty's Secrets: The Lost Wisdom of America's Founders* (New York: WND Books, 2015), 89.
118. Mark R. Levin, *Unfreedom of the Press* (New York: Threshold Editions, 2019), 61.
119. *Ibid.*, 60.
120. *Ibid.*, 61.
121. Ronald Pestritto, "Woodrow Wilson: Godfather of Liberalism," *Heritage Foundation*, July 31, 2012, https://www.heritage.org/political-process/report/woodrow-wilson-godfather-liberalism.
122. Tiffany Jones Miller, "Progressivism, Race, and the Training Wheels of Freedom," *National Review*, November 14, 2011, 38.
123. Paul Roderick Gregory, "Why the Fuss? Obama Has Long Been on Record in Favor of Redistribution," *Forbes*, September 23, 2012, https://www.forbes.com/sites/paulroderickgregory/2012/09/23/why-the-fuss-obama-has-long-been-on-record-in-favor-of-redistribution/#1ca3a675593a.
124. *Ibid.*
125. Remarks of President Donald Trump at the 2018 National Prayer Breakfast held at the Washington Hilton Hotel, Washington, D.C. on February 8, 2018. "Remarks by President Trump at the 66th Annual National Prayer Breakfast," February 8, 2018, https://www.whitehouse.gov/briefings-statements/remarks-president-trump-66th-annual-national-prayer-breakfast/.
126. David W. Southern, *The Progressive Era and Race: Reaction and Reform, 1900-1917* (Wheeling: Harlan Davidson, Inc., 2005), 88.
127. *Ibid.*, 133.
128. *Ibid.*, 103.

129. "Hillary Clinton Honored with the Woodrow Wilson Award for Public Service," Wilson Center, April 26, 2012, https://www.wilsoncenter.org/event/hillary-clinton-honored-the-woodrow-wilson-award-for-public-service.
130. Steven F. Hayward, "Now That Hillary Clinton Has Dismissed 'Liberalism,' Can Conservatives Take It Back?," *Forbes*, December 11, 2013, https://www.forbes.com/sites/stevenhayward/2013/12/11/now-that-hillary-clinton-has-dismissed-liberalism-can-conservatives-take-it-back/#1415cb6d221f.
131. David Azerrad, "The Good Ol' Progressive Contempt for the Founding," *Daily Signal*, May 14, 2013, https://www.dailysignal.com/2013/05/14/the-good-ol-progressive-contempt-for-the-founding/.
132. Arina Grossu, "Margaret Sanger: Racist Eugenicist Extraordinaire," *Washington Times*, May 5, 2014.
133. George Grant, *Killer Angel: A Short Biography of Planned Parenthood's Founder, Margaret Sanger* (Nashville: Cumberland House Publishing, 1995), 83.
134. David W. Southern, *The Progressive Era and Race: Reaction and Reform, 1900-1917* (Wheeling: Harlan Davidson, Inc., 2005), 50.
135. Jamie Dean, "Against the Tide," *World Magazine*, January 19, 2019, 36.
136. "Democrat Legislator Demands Black Babies Be Exempt from Heartbeat Laws," Pulpit & Pen, April 20, 2019, https://pulpitandpen.org/2019/04/20/democrat-legislator-demands-black-babies-be-exempt-from-heartbeat-laws/.
137. *Ibid.*
138. Steven W. Mosher, "The Repackaging of Margaret Sanger," *Wall Street Journal*, May 5, 1997, https://www.wsj.com/articles/SB862769009690799000.
139. Margaret Sanger, *An Autobiography* (New York: W.W. Norton & Company, 1938), 366.
140. "Planned Parenthood Honors Hillary Clinton with Margaret Sanger Award," March 27, 2009, https://www.sba-list.org/newsroom/news/planned-parenthood-honors-hillary-clinton-margaret-sanger-award.
141. Katie Reilly, "Hillary Clinton's 'Basket of Deplorables' Remarks about Donald Trump Supporters," *Time*, September 10, 2016, http://time.com/4486502/hillary-clinton-basket-of-deplorables-transcript/.
142. George Grant, *Killer Angel: A Short Biography of Planned Parenthood's Founder, Margaret Sanger* (Nashville: Cumberland House Publishing, 1995), 62.
143. David W. Southern, *The Progressive Era and Race: Reaction and Reform, 1900-1917* (Wheeling: Harlan Davidson, Inc., 2005), 50.
144. Carly Hoilman, "VA Governor Supports Post-Birth Infanticide in Shocking Radio Interview," Faithwire, January 30, 2019, https://www.faithwire.com/2019/01/30/va-governor-supports-post-birth-infanticide-in-shocking-radio-interview/.

145. "Trump Jumps into Virginia Uproar over Late-Term Abortion," *Associated Press*, January 30, 2019, https://www.nbcnews.com/politics/politics-news/virginia-democratic-governor-touches-abortion-uproar-n964896.

CHAPTER 5, TWENTY-FIRST-CENTURY DEMOCRATS

146. "Abortion Surveillance-United States," Centers for Disease Control and Prevention, 2011, http://www.cdc.gov/mmwr/preview/mmwrhtml/ss6311a1.htm?s_cid=ss6311a1_w.
147. *Ibid.*
148. *Ibid.*
149. Monica Burke, "New Report Shows Planned Parenthood Raked in $1.5 Billion in Taxpayer Funds over 3 Years," *Heritage Foundation*, March 12, 2018, https://www.heritage.org/marriage-and-family/commentary/new-report-shows-planned-parenthood-raked-15-billion-taxpayer-funds.
150. "Racial Targeting Report," Life Dynamics, http://www.maafa21.com/racial-targeting-report.
151. Arthur Goldberg, "Abortion's Devastating Impact upon Black Americans," *Public Discourse: The Journal of the Witherspoon Institute*, February 11, 2019, https://www.thepublicdiscourse.com/2019/02/48594/.
152. "Planned Parenthood," OpenSecrets.org, https://www.opensecrets.org/orgs/totals.php?id=D000000591&cycle=2016.
153. *Ibid.*
154. Tommy Schultz, "National School Choice Poll: 63% of Likely 2018 Voters Support School Choice," American Federation for Children, January 18, 2018.
155. "Center for Responsive Politics, National Education Association," OpenSecrets.org, https://www.opensecrets.org/orgs/summary.php?id=D000000064.
156. Peter Roff, "Obama Wrong on DC Vouchers and Hypocritical, Just Like Congress, US News & World Reports," *Jefferson Street* (blog), April 22, 2009.
157. Jason L. Riley, "The Blue Wave May Wash Education Reform Away," *Wall Street Journal*, November 13, 2018.
158. Doha Madani, "'I'd take the wall down,' says Beto O'Rourke of current border barriers," *NBC News*, February 14, 2019, https://www.nbcnews.com/news/us-news/i-d-take-wall-down-says-beto-o-rourke-current-n971896.
159. Kayla Fontenot, Jessica Semega, and Melissa Kollar, "Income and Poverty in the United States: 2017," U.S. Census Bureau publication, September 2018, 12, table 3.
160. Editorial Board, "Yes, Democrats Want Higher Gas Prices and Other Comments," *New York Post*, June 1, 2018, https://nypost.com/2018/06/01/yes-democrats-want-higher-gas-prices-and-other-comments/.
161. Chris Pummer, "$8-a-Gallon Gas," *Wall Street Journal Market Watch*, May 28, 2008, https://www.marketwatch.com/story/eight-reasons-youll-rejoice-we.

162. Jude Clemente, "Higher Cost Energy Worsens the Shameful Rise in American Poverty," *Forbes*, September 21, 2015.
163. Nick Cunningham, "Trump's Ultimate Move to Lower Gasoline Prices," OilPrice.com, July 16, 2018, https://oilprice.com/Energy/Gas-Prices/Trumps-Ultimate-Move-To-Lower-Gasoline-Prices.html.
164. Daniel Cox, Rachel Lienesch, and Robert P. Jones, "Who Sees Discrimination? Attitudes on Sexual Orientation, Gender Identity, Race, and Immigration Status: Findings from PRRI's American Values Atlas," June 21, 2017, https://www.prri.org/research/americans-views-discrimination-immigrants-blacks-lgbt-sex-marriage-immigration-reform/.
165. *Ibid.*
166. Karl Vick and Ashley Surdin, "Most of California's Black Voters Backed Gay Marriage Ban," *Washington Post*, November 7, 2008.
167. Daniel Cox, Rachel Lienesch, and Robert P. Jones, "Who Sees Discrimination? Attitudes on Sexual Orientation, Gender Identity, Race, and Immigration Status: Findings from PRRI's American Values Atlas," June 21, 2017, https://www.prri.org/research/americans-views-discrimination-immigrants-blacks-lgbt-sex-marriage-immigration-reform/.
168. Walter Williams, "Economic Conspiracies," *Casper Star Tribune*, August 29, 2016, https://trib.com/opinion/columns/williams-economic-conspiracies/article_3204aab1-5a5c-53d8-a96f-84d4e6ef35be.html.
169. Marcus Cole, "Medallion Monopoly Drives Taxicab Racism," Institute for Justice, February 2000, https://ij.org/ll/february-2000-volume-9-number-1/medallion-monopoly-drives-taxicab-racism/.
170. Gabrielle Pickard-Whitehead, "Wow! American Small Business Ownership Up 400% in a Year, Survey Reveals," Small Business Trends, August 9, 2018, https://smallbiztrends.com/2018/08/african-american-small-business-statistics-2018.html.
171. David W. Southern, *The Progressive Era and Race: Reaction and Reform, 1900-1917* (Wheeling: Harlan Davidson, Inc., 2005), 24.

CHAPTER 6, LYNDON JOHNSON

172. Robert A. Caro, *Master of the Senate: The Years of Lyndon Johnson* (New York: Alfred A Knopf, 2013), xvi.
173. *Ibid.*
174. *Ibid.*, 116.
175. *Ibid.*, xvi.
176. *Ibid.*, xx.
177. *Ibid.*, 715.
178. Ronnie Dugger, *The Politician: The Life and Times of Lyndon Johnson* (Toronto: George J. McLeod Limited, 1982), 310.
179. Robert Parker, *Capitol Hill in Black and White* (New York: Dodd, Mead & Company, 1986), v.

180. Robert A. Caro, *Master of the Senate: The Years of Lyndon Johnson* (New York: Alfred A Knopf, 2013), 842-843.
181. Chester J. Pach, Jr., and Elmo Richardson, *The Presidency of Dwight D. Eisenhower* (Lawrence: University Press of Kansas, 1991), 153.
182. Robert A. Caro, *Master of the Senate: The Years of Lyndon Johnson* (New York: Alfred A Knopf, 2013), 863.
183. *Ibid.*, 715.
184. Ronnie Dugger, *The Politician: The Life and Times of Lyndon Johnson* (New York: W.W. Norton & Company, 1982), 91.
185. Robert A. Caro, *Master of the Senate: The Years of Lyndon Johnson* (New York: Alfred A Knopf, 2013), 712.
186. Ronald Kessler, *Inside the White House* (New York: Simon & Schuster, 1995), 33.
187. Robert A. Caro, *Master of the Senate: The Years of Lyndon Johnson* (New York: Alfred A Knopf, 2013), 712.
188. Scott Van Wynsberghe, "The Most Vulgar American President Ever? It Sure as #$@!%* Isn't Donald Trump," *National Post*, January 26, 2018, https://nationalpost.com/opinion/the-most-vulgar-american-president-ever-it-sure-as-isnt-donald-trump.
189. Robert Parker, *Capitol Hill in Black and White* (New York: Dodd, Mead & Company, 1986), 213.
190. Ronald Kessler, *Inside the White House* (New York: Simon & Schuster, 1995), 33.
191. This story was related to Bruce Eberle by one of the gentlemen to which this story was told, but since the high-profile journalist is no longer living, the person who related the story to Bruce asked that the gentleman who was invited to the Johnson ranch and experienced this immoral behavior by Lyndon Johnson not be identified.
192. Robert A. Caro, *Master of the Senate: The Years of Lyndon Johnson* (New York: Alfred A Knopf, 2013), 141, 144, 145.
193. *Ibid.*, 115, 116.
194. *Ibid.*, 227, 228.

CHAPTER 7, BARRY GOLDWATER

195. Theodore H. White, *The Making of the President 1964* (New York: HarperCollins Publishers, 1965), 201.
196. Gary A Donaldson, *Liberalism's Last Hurrah: The Presidential Campaign of 1964* (New York: Skyhorse Publishing, 2002), back cover.
197. *Ibid.*, 293.
198. Lionel Lokos, *Hysteria 1964: The Fear Campaign Against Barry Goldwater* (New Rochelle: Arlington House, 1967), dust cover.
199. *Ibid.*, 123.
200. *Ibid.*, 127.
201. *Ibid.*, 145.
202. *Ibid.*, 149.
203. *Ibid.*, 165.

204. Bart Barnes, "Barry Goldwater, GOP Hero, Dies," *Washington Post*, May 30, 1998, https://www.washingtonpost.com/wp-srv/politics/daily/may98/goldwater30.htm.
205. Bob Wood and Dean Smith, *Barry Goldwater* (New York: Avon Book Division, The Hearst Corporation, 1961), 20-49.
206. J. William Middendorf II, *A Glorious Disaster: Barry Goldwater's Presidential Campaign and the Origins of the Conservative Movement* (New York: Basic Books, 2006), 106.
207. Barry Goldwater with Jack Casserly, *Goldwater* (New York: Doubleday, 1988), 173.
208. Lee Edwards, *Goldwater: The Man Who Made a Revolution* (Washington, D.C.: Regnery Publishing, Inc., 1995), 29.
209. *Ibid.*, 28.
210. Robert Alan Goldberg, *Barry Goldwater* (New Haven: Yale University Press, 1995), 89; US Inflation Calculator, https://www.usinflationcalculator.com/. In 2019 dollars, Goldwater donated the equivalent of $3,947.25 to the 1951 NAACP drive to integrate Phoenix public schools.
211. Lee Edwards, *Goldwater: The Man Who Made a Revolution* (Washington, D.C.: Regnery Publishing, Inc., 1995), 38.
212. *Ibid.*, 49–50.
213. *Ibid.*, 45.
214. *Ibid.*, 231.
215. *Ibid.*
216. "U.S. Inflation Rate, $200 in 1952 to 2019," CPI Inflation Calculator, http://www.in2013dollars.com/us/inflation/1952?amount=200. According to the Bureau of Labor Statistics consumer price index, today's prices in 2019 are 859.25% higher than average prices throughout 1952. $200 in 1952 is equivalent in purchasing power to about $1,918.51 in 2019, a difference of $1,718.51 over 67 years.
217. Lee Edwards, *Goldwater: The Man Who Made a Revolution* (Washington, D.C.: Regnery Publishing, Inc., 1995), 231.
218. *Ibid.*, 232.
219. Lee Edwards, "In Barry Goldwater, the Conscience of a Conservative," *Miami Herald*, July 2, 2014, https://www.miamiherald.com/latest-news/article1973798.html.
220. Lee Edwards, *Goldwater: The Man Who Made a Revolution* (Washington, D.C.: Regnery Publishing, Inc., 1995), 231.
221. Barry Goldwater with Jack Casserly, *Goldwater* (New York: Doubleday, 1998), 172.
222. As related to Bruce Eberle by Lee Edwards on multiple occasions.
223. Lee Edwards, "In Barry Goldwater, the Conscience of a Conservative," *Miami Herald*, July 2, 2014, https://www.miamiherald.com/latest-news/article1973798.html.
224. As related to Bruce Eberle by Lee Edwards on July 10, 2018. Edwards served as Press Secretary to Barry Goldwater in 1964 when this event

occurred and saw a copy of the 75-page opinion furnished to Goldwater regarding the Civil Rights Act of 1964.

225. This trail of inquiry by Goldwater into the constitutionality of the Civil Rights Act of 1964 was related to Bruce Eberle by Lee Edwards, who served as Goldwater's Press Secretary at that time. This conversation took place on June 10, 2018.
226. Arnold L. Steinberg, *Whiplash!: From JFK to Donald Trump, a Political Odyssey* (Ottawa: Jameson Books, Inc., 2017), 109; Harry Stein, "The Goldwater Takedown," *City Journal* (Autumn 2016).
227. Lee Edwards, *Goldwater: The Man Who Made a Revolution* (Washington, D.C.: Regnery Publishing, Inc., 1995), 231.
228. Allan Brownfeld in a telephone conversation with Bruce Eberle on June 19, 2019.
229. *Ibid.*, 246.

CHAPTER 8, CIVIL RIGHTS PIONEERS

230. Wayne Thorburn, *A Generation Awakes: Young Americans for Freedom and the Creation of the Conservative Movement* (Ottawa: Jameson Books, Inc., 2010), 111.
231. Bruce Eberle, who served on the national board of directors of Young Americans for Freedom from 1967 to 1971, and previously served as Missouri Chairman of YAF, then later as a member of the board of directors of Texas Young Americans for Freedom, made this observation.
232. David A. Nichols, *A Matter of Justice: Eisenhower and the Beginning of the Civil Rights Revolution* (New York: Simon & Schuster, 2007), 1.
233. *Ibid.*, 11-12.
234. *Ibid.*, 9.
235. *Ibid.*
236. *Ibid.*, 9-10.
237. *Ibid.*, 6.
238. *Ibid.*, 190.
239. The Civil Rights Bill of 1956 was defeated thorough an effort orchestrated by Lyndon Johnson.
240. "Executive Order 9981," Wikipedia, https://en.wikipedia.org/wiki/Executive_Order_9981. Executive Order 9981 is an executive order issued on July 26, 1948, by President Harry S. Truman. It abolished discrimination "on the basis of race, color, religion or national origin" in the United States Armed Forces.
241. David A. Nichols, *A Matter of Justice: Eisenhower and the Beginning of the Civil Rights Revolution* (New York: Simon & Schuster, 2007), 26.
242. *Ibid.*, 34.
243. Timothy M. Thurber, *Republicans and Race: The GOP's Frayed Relationship with African Americans, 1945-1974* (Lawrence: University Press of Kansas, 2013), 85.
244. Chester J. Pach, Jr., and Elmo Richardson, *The Presidency of Dwight D. Eisenhower* (Lawrence: University Press of Kansas, 1991), 153.

245. Jonathan Aitken, *Nixon: A Life* (Washington, D.C.: Regnery Publishing, Inc., 1993), 72.
246. *Ibid.*
247. *Ibid.*, 247.
248. Robert A. Caro, *Master of the Senate: The Years of Lyndon Johnson* (New York: Alfred A Knopf, 2013), 988.
249. Jonathan Aitken, *Nixon: A Life* (Washington, D.C.: Regnery Publishing, Inc., 1993), 248.
250. *Ibid.*, 281.
251. Shaun A. Casey, *The Making of a Catholic President: Kennedy vs. Nixon 1960* (New York: Oxford University Press, 2009), 194.
252. Jonathan Aitken, *Nixon: A Life* (Washington, D.C.: Regnery Publishing, Inc., 1993), 281.
253. Shaun A. Casey, *The Making of a Catholic President: Kennedy vs. Nixon 1960* (New York: Oxford University Press, 2009), 194.
254. Jonathan Aitken, *Nixon: A Life* (Washington, D.C.: Regnery Publishing, Inc., 1993), 281.
255. Theodore R. Johnson, "What Nixon Can Teach the GOP about Courting Black Voters," *Politico Magazine*, August 15, 2015, https://www.politico.com/magazine/story/2015/08/what-nixon-can-teach-the-gop-about-courting-black-voters-121392.
256. Jonathan Aitken, *Nixon: A Life* (Washington, D.C.: Regnery Publishing, Inc., 1993), 394.
257. *Ibid.*
258. "Nixon's Record on Civil Rights," Nixon Foundation, August 4, 2017, https://www.nixonfoundation.org/2017/08/nixons-record-civil-rights-2/.
259. Ronald Reagan, *An American Life* (New York: Simon & Schuster, 1990), 30.
260. *Ibid.*, 52.
261. *Ibid.*
262. *Ibid.*
263. Raymond Wolters, *Right Turn: William Bradford Reynolds, the Reagan Administration, and Black Civil Rights* (New Brunswick: Transaction Publishers, 1996), 3.
264. Craig Shirley, "A Point by Point Rebuttal on Reagan and Racism," *Newsmax*, August 14, 2019, https://www.newsmax.com/craigshirley/ronald-reagan-racism/2019/08/14/id/928557/.
265. Benny Johnson, "Black Unemployment Plunges to Record Low, Gap between White, Black Unemployment Smallest in History," *Daily Caller*, June 1, 2018, https://dailycaller.com/2018/06/01/black-unemployment-plunges-to-record-low-gap-between-white-black-unemployment-smallest-in-history/.
266. "Real Wages Are Rising," *Wall Street Journal*, September 7, 2018, https://www.wsj.com/articles/real-wages-are-rising-1536359667.
267. *Ibid.*
268. Mola Lenghi, "More than 3,000 Prisoners Released under First Step Act," *CBS Evening News*, July 19, 2019, https://www.cbsnews.com/news/

first-step-act-thousands-released-from-prisons-halfway-houses-today -2019-07-19/.

269. Steven Nelson, "Trump Announces Second Step Act to Help Ex-prisoners Find Work," *Washington Examiner*, April 1, 2019, https://www .washingtonexaminer.com/news/white-house/trump-announces-second -step-act-to-help-ex-prisoners-find-work.
270. "President Trump Signs First Step Act Legislation-'Makes America Safer,'" Prison Fellowship, December 21, 2018.
271. "Remarks by President Trump at the White House Opportunity and Revitalization Council Meeting," April 4, 2019, https://www.whitehouse .gov/briefings-statements/remarks-president-trump-white-house -opportunity-revitalization-council-meeting/.
272. "For instance, at the Department of Energy, because of what we're seeing and the growth in the energy industry, a truck driver that—we need a great deal of truck drivers in the Bakken or in Louisiana or over in the Permian Basin—those truck drivers being able to shift over from a year ago being in prison, to—through one of these reentry programs, into an Opportunity Zone, a job driving a truck, making $100,000 a year, Sonny [Perdue]. I mean, that's—you talk about transformational for a family. That's what we're looking at here." Comments by Department of Energy Secretary Rick Perry, "Remarks by President Trump at the White House Opportunity and Revitalization Council Meeting," April 4, 2019, https://www.whitehouse .gov/briefings-statements/remarks-president-trump-white-house -opportunity-revitalization-council-meeting/.
273. "President Trump Signs First Step Act Legislation-'Makes America Safer'," Prison Fellowship, December 21, 2018.
274. Ian Schwartz, "Pastor Darrell Scott: Trump Most Pro-black President in My Lifetime," RealClear Politics, August 3, 2018, https://www.realclear politics.com/video/2018/08/03/pastor_darrell_scott_trump_most_ pro-black_president_in_my_lifetime.html.

CHAPTER 9, TAKING ACTION

275. Jackie Robinson later switched to the Democratic Party when Barry Goldwater voted against the Civil Rights Act of 1964, but he was a registered Republican at the time he broke the color barrier of major league baseball.
276. Lee Lowenfish, *Branch Rickey: Baseball's Ferocious Gentleman* (Lincoln: University of Nebraska Press, 2007), 9.
277. Jesse Washington, "Jackie Robinson's Contracts with Brooklyn Dodgers, Montreal Royals Set for Display," ESPN, April 14, 2016, http://www.espn .com/mlb/story/_/id/15171202/jackie-robinson-contracts-brooklyn -dodgers-montreal-royals-set-display-valued-36-million.
278. "Gentleman's Agreement: A Brief History of Negro League Baseball in America," Marin Theatre Company, https://www.marintheatre.org/ productions/fences/fences-negro-leagues. Although Jackie Robinson is widely remembered as the first African American to play on an all-white

major league baseball team, a number of black players played alongside whites on both minor and major league teams in the decades just after the inception of professional baseball. Some of these players even managed to build relatively long careers during this time. The best black players found tolerance, if not acceptance, in white baseball in the North and the Midwest through the 1880s. But this changed drastically in 1890, as baseball was rapidly becoming the national sport. Without a formal rule or announcement, a "gentleman's agreement" had been struck that would cement the baseball color barrier for the next fifty-five years, and within just a few years no team in organized baseball would draft black players.

279. *Ibid.*
280. Vince Staten, *Ol' Diz: A Biography of Dizzy Dean* (New York: Harper Collins Publishers 1992), 171.
281. *Ibid.*
282. *Ibid.*
283. "Negro League Baseball," Wikipedia, https://en.wikipedia.org/wiki/Negro_league_baseball. On February 13 and 14, 1920, talks were held in Kansas City, Missouri at the YMCA that established the Negro National League and its governing body the National Association of Colored Professional Base Ball Clubs. The league was initially composed of eight teams: Chicago American Giants, Chicago Giants, Cuban Stars, Dayton Marcos, Detroit Stars, Indianapolis ABC's, Kansas City Monarchs and St. Louis Giants. Rube Foster was named league president.
284. Branch Rickey to Frank Stanton, January 18, 1949.
285. Murray Polner, *Branch Rickey: A Biography* (Fairfield: Fairfield Graphics, 1982), 207.
286. Proverbs 27.2, God's Word translation, Holy Bible.
287. Ed Henry, *42 Faith: The Rest of the Jackie Robinson Story* (Nashville: HarperCollins Publishers, 2017), 59.
288. Lee Lowenfish, *Branch Rickey: Baseball's Ferocious Gentleman* (Lincoln: University of Nebraska Press, 2007), 305.
289. *Ibid.*, 273, 290, 305, 351.
290. *Ibid.*, 518.
291. *Ibid.*, 518.
292. Arnold Rampersad, *Jackie Robinson: A Biography* (New York: Ballantine Publishing Group, 1997), 122.
293. Ed Henry, *42 Faith: The Rest of the Jackie Robinson Story* (Nashville: HarperCollins Publishers, 2017), 32.
294. Lee Lowenfish, *Branch Rickey: Baseball's Ferocious Gentleman* (Lincoln: University of Nebraska Press, 2007), 123.
295. Ed Henry, *42 Faith: The Rest of the Jackie Robinson Story* (Nashville: HarperCollins Publishers, 2017), 87.
296. Murray Polner, *Branch Rickey: A Biography* (Fairfield: Fairfield Graphics, 1982), 167.
297. *Ibid.*, 167.
298. *Ibid.*

299. Ed Henry, *42 Faith: The Rest of the Jackie Robinson Story* (Nashville: HarperCollins Publishers, 2017), 85.
300. Richard A. Serrano, "Dodgers Sign a Negro," Kansas City Times, October 23, 1945, https://www.kansascity.com/latest-news/article295387/DODGERS-SIGN-A-NEGRO.html.
301. Lee Lowenfish, *Branch Rickey: Baseball's Ferocious Gentleman* (Lincoln: University of Nebraska Press, 2007), 311.
302. Ed Henry, *42 Faith: The Rest of the Jackie Robinson Story* (Nashville: HarperCollins Publishers, 2017), 61.
303. William C. Kashatus, "Martin Luther King Inspired by Jackie Robinson," *Philadelphia Inquirer*, January 18, 1997, http://www.historylive.net/op-eds-bill-kashatus/martin-luther-king-inspired-by-jackie-robinson/.
304. Lee Lowenfish, *Branch Rickey: Baseball's Ferocious Gentleman* (Lincoln: University of Nebraska Press, 2007), 194.

CHAPTER 10, MALICIOUS FALSE NARRATIVE

305. "Nixon's Record on Civil Rights," Nixon Foundation, August 4, 2017, https://www.nixonfoundation.org/2017/08/nixons-record-civil-rights-2/.
306. Orval Faubus, "Governor Blocked School Desegregation," *Los Angeles Times*, December 15, 1994.
307. "Bull Connor," Wikipedia, https://en.wikipedia.org/wiki/Bull_Connor.
308. "The Declaration of Constitutional Principles (known informally as the Southern Manifesto) was a document written in February and March 1956, in opposition to racial integration of public places." "Southern Manifesto," Wikipedia, https://en.wikipedia.org/wiki/Southern_Manifesto.
309. R.W. Apple, Jr., "J. William Fulbright, Senate Giant, Is Dead at 89," *New York Times*, February 10, 1995.
310. *Ibid.*
311. Chris Richards, "Is Trump Sending a Message by Awarding the Medal of Freedom to Elvis? Yes.," *Washington Post*, November 15, 2018.
312. *Washington Post*, J. William Fulbright Obituary, https://www.washingtonpost.com/archive/opinions/1995/02/10/j-william-fulbright/4a7578c7-c6c4-440f-be81-b780ace31e0b/?utm_term=.4e9807b0bacf.
313. Gerard Alexander, "The Myth of the Racist Republicans," Claremont Institute, March 20, 2004, https://www.claremont.org/crb/article/the-myth-of-the-racist-republicans/.
314. *Ibid.*
315. *Ibid.*
316. Ann Coulter, *Mugged: Racial Demagoguery from the Seventies to Obama* (New York: Sentinel, 2012), 171.
317. Earl Black and Merle Black, *The Rise of Southern Republicans* (Cambridge: Belknap Press/Harvard University Press, 2002), 93.
318. Gerard Alexander, "The Myth of the Racist Republicans," Claremont Institute, March 20, 2004, https://www.claremont.org/crb/article/the-myth-of-the-racist-republicans/.

319. Richard H. Rovere, "The Campaign: Goldwater," *New Yorker*, September 25, 1964, https://www.newyorker.com/magazine/1964/10/03/the-campaign-goldwater.
320. Lee Edwards, *Goldwater: The Man Who Made A Revolution* (Washington, D.C.: Regnery Publishing, Inc., 1995), 332–333.
321. *Ibid.*
322. Jonathan Aitken, *Nixon: A Life* (Washington, D.C.: Regnery Publishing, Inc., 1993), 394.
323. Daniel DiSalvo, "The Great Re-migration," *City Journal* (Summer 2012).
324. William H. Frey, *Diversity Explosion: How New Racial Demographics are Remaking America* (Washington, D.C.: Brookings Institution Press, 2018), 3.
325. "Black Migration Is Now from North to South," Black Entertainment Network, March 24, 2014, https://www.bet.com/news/national/2014/03/24/black-migration-is-now-from-north-to-south.html.
326. *Ibid.*
327. Carmen K. Sisson, "Why African-Americans Are Moving Back to the South," *Christian Science Monitor*, March 16, 2014.
328. *Ibid.*
329. Rodney Hawkins, "Biden Tells African-American Audience GOP Ticket Would Put Them 'Back in Chains'," *CBS News*, August 14, 2012, https://www.cbsnews.com/news/biden-tells-african-american-audience-gop-ticket-would-put-them-back-in-chains/.
330. Meg Kinnard and Bill Barrow, "Biden: Trump, Republicans Allowing Jim Crow to Return," *Associated Press*, May 4, 2019, https://www.apnews.com/2eda3c2355fe45408422fb5f7f5e2522.
331. Stephen Moore, "Trump's Real Record on Race May Surprise You," *Chicago Tribune*, August 21, 2017, https://www.chicagotribune.com/news/opinion/commentary/ct-perspec-race-trump-economy-progress-0822-story.html.
332. Jason L. Riley, "Among Black Voters, Trump's Popularity Inches Upward," *Wall Street Journal*, November 6, 2018.

CHAPTER 11, ABANDONMENT

333. Brentin Mock, "What Police and Poor Communities Really Think of Each Other," CityLab, February 23, 2017, https://www.citylab.com/equity/2017/02/how-poor-communities-view-the-police/517485/.
334. "Police Release 2018 Shooting Numbers," *Chicago Sun Times*, January 1, 2019, https://chicago.suntimes.com/news/police-2018-shooting-data/.
335. Katherine Rosenberg-Douglas and Hannah Leone, "As Cold Weather Breaks, Violence Returns: 24 Shot in 30 Hours over Warmest Weekend This Year," *Chicago Tribune*, April 8, 2019, https://www.chicagotribune.com/news/local/breaking/ct-met-citywide-shootings-20190407-story.html.
336. "Police Release 2018 Shooting Numbers," *Chicago Sun Times*, January 1, 2019, https://chicago.suntimes.com/news/police-2018-shooting-data/.
337. *Ibid.*

338. Anne Gearan and Abby Phillip, "Clinton Regrets 1996 Remark on 'Super Predators' after Encounter with Activist," *Washington Post*, February 25, 2016, https://www.washingtonpost.comnews/post-politics/wp/2016/02/25/clinton-heckled-by-black-lives-matter-activist/?utm_term=.7fffa05db65a.
339. Robert Rector, "How Welfare Undermines Marriage and What to Do about It," *Heritage Foundation*, November 17, 2014, https://www.heritage.org/welfare/report/how-welfare-undermines-marriage-and-what-do-about-it.
340. Joyce A. Martin, M.P.H. et al., "Births: Final Data for 2017," Centers for Disease Control and Prevention, National Vital Statistics Report 67, no. 8 (November 7, 2018).
341. Crystal Wright, "How Liberal Policies Destroyed Black Families," *Daily Signal*, March 29, 2016, https://www.dailysignal.com/2016/03/29/how-liberal-policies-destroyed-black-families/.
342. Kay S. Hymowitz, "The Black Family: 40 Years of Lies," *City Journal* (Summer 2005), https://www.city-journal.org/html/black-family-40-years-lies-12872.html.
343. United States Census Bureau, July 1, 2018, https://www.census.gov/quickfacts/fact/table/US/PST045218.
344. *Ibid.*
345. Paul Bedard, "New Border Surge Prompts 10% Jump in 2019 Prediction to 1,072,000 Illegal Immigrants," *Washington Examiner*, June 6, 2019, https://www.washingtonexaminer.com/washington-secrets/new-border-surge-prompts-10-jump-in-2019-prediction-to-1-072-000-illegal-immigrants.
346. Gregg Re, "Beto O'Rourke Says He 'Absolutely' Supports Destroying Existing Walls on Southern Border," *Fox News*, February 14, 2019, https://www.foxnews.com/politics/beto-orourke-says-he-absolutely-supports-destroying-existing-walls-on-southern-border.
347. Spencer P. Morrison, "Illegal Immigration Hurts Black Workers Most," American Thinker, August 13, 2019, https://www.americanthinker.com/articles/2019/08/illegal_immigration_hurts_black_workers_most.html.
348. Rebecca Savransky, "Obama to Trump: 'What Magic Wand Do You Have?'," *The Hill*, June 1, 2018, https://thehill.com/blogs/blog-briefing-room/news/281936-obama-to-trump-what-magic-wand-do-you-have.
349. Adam Shaw, "Thousands of French Protesters Clash with Police, Call for Macron's Resignation over Gas Taxes," *Fox News*, November 24, 2018, https://www.foxnews.com/world/thousands-of-french-police-use-tear-gas-water-cannon-against-paris-protesters.
350. "Sustainable Development Goals," United Nations, December 14, 2015, https://www.un.org/sustainabledevelopment/blog/2015/12/2-billion-move-out-of-extreme-poverty-over-25-years-says-un-report/.
351. Bradley Blakeman, "Green New Deal Will Change America for the Worst, Killing Jobs, Livestock and Airline Industries," *Fox News*, https://www.foxnews.com/opinion/bradley-blakeman-green-new-deal-will-change-america-for-the-worst-killing-jobs-livestock-and-airline-industries.
352. *Ibid.*

353. Ledyard King, "Green New Deal Too Ambitious for Some Democrats, Even Those Who Say Congress Must 'Do Something'," *USA Today*, March 7, 2019, https://www.usatoday.com/story/news/politics/2019/03/07/green-new-deal-not-all-democrats-board-ambitious-climate-plan/3032887002/.
354. John T. Bennett, "White House Black Leadership Event Turns into Mini-Trump Rally," Roll Call, October 26, 2018, https://www.rollcall.com/news/politics/white-house-black-leadership-event-turns-mini-trump-rally.

CHAPTER 12, LEFT-TO-RIGHT ODYSSEY

355. David W. Southern, *The Progressive Era and Race: Reaction and Reform, 1900–1917* (Wheeling: Harlan Davidson, Inc., 2005), 24.
356. As related to son Vernon Robinson by his mother, Stella Pecot Robinson.
357. *Ibid.*

CHAPTER 13, DISILLUSIONED

358. Rodd Dreher, "Democrats: Open Borders 4-Evah," *American Conservative*, June 28, 2019, https://www.theamericanconservative.com/dreher/democrats-open-borders/.
359. Star Parker, "The Effects of Abortion on the Black Community," Center for Urban Renewal and Education, June 2015.
360. David Harsanyi, "Reminder: Democrats Want to Raise Your Gas Prices on Purpose," *Real Clear Politics*, June 1, 2018, https://www.realclearpolitics.com/articles/2018/06/01/why_arent_liberals_celebrating_higher_gas_prices_its_what_they_want_137171.html.
361. Salena Zito, "Democrats Still Haven't Faced Their God Problem," *New York Post*, March 15, 2017, https://nypost.com/2017/03/15/democrats-still-havent-faced-their-god-problem/.
362. David Harsanyi, "The Democrats' Fight against School Choice Is Immoral," Reason, January 20, 2017, https://reason.com/2017/01/20/the-democrats-fight-against-school-choic/.
363. Larry Elder, "Public School Teachers and Democrat Politicians Send Their Own Kids to Private Schools," Wintery Knight, October 18, 2013, https://winteryknight.com/2013/10/18/public-school-teachers-and-democrat-politicians-send-their-own-kids-to-private-schools/, excerpted from *Investors Business Daily*, October 16, 2013.
364. "Republicans Pass Historic Tax Cuts without a Single Democratic Vote," *Axios*, December 20, 2017, https://www.axios.com/republicans-pass-historic-tax-cuts-without-a-single-democratic-vote-1515110718-8cdf005c-c1c9-481a-975b-72336765ebe4.html.
365. Stephen Moore, "Trump's Real Record on Race May Surprise You," *Chicago Tribune*, August 21, 2017, https://www.chicagotribune.com/news/opinion/commentary/ct-perspec-race-trump-economy-progress-0822-story.html.
366. Erin McCarthy Holliday, "President Trump Signs Criminal Justice Reform First Step Act into Law," *Jurist*, December 21, 2018, https://

www.jurist.org/news/2018/12/president-trump-signs-criminal-justice-reform-first-step-act-into-law/.

367. Alex Murashko, "DNC: Christian Leaders Comment on Night 'Dems Booed God'," *Christian Post*, September 7, 2012, https://www.christianpost.com/news/dnc-christian-leaders-comment-on-night-dems-booed-god.html.
368. David Masci, "5 Facts about the Religious Lives of African Americans," Pew Research Center, February 7, 2018, https://www.pewresearch.org/fact-tank/2018/02/07/5-facts-about-the-religious-lives-of-african-americans/.
369. Alex Daniels, "Religious Americans Give More, New Study Finds," Chronicle of Philanthropy, November 25, 2013, https://www.philanthropy.com/article/Religious-Americans-Give-More/153973.
370. Victor Davis Hanson, *The Case for Trump* (New York: Basic Books, 2019), 187.
371. "Pennsylvania Statewide," Axiom Strategies, www.RemingtonResearchGroup.com. Survey conducted November 1 through November 2, 2016. 2,683 likely General Election voters participated in the survey. Survey weighted to match expected turnout demographics for the 2016 General Election. Margin of Error is ±1.89% with a 95% level of confidence. Totals do not always equal 100% due to rounding.
372. Michael Moore, "5 Reasons Why Trump Will Win," MichaelMoore, https://michaelmoore.com/trumpwillwin/.
373. "Voting and Registration in the Election of November 2016," United States Census Bureau, May 2017, table 2, https://www.census.gov/data/tables/time-series/demo/voting-and-registration/p20-580.html. Number arrived at by multiplying the number of registered black Americans who voted by 8%, the percent of the black vote commonly attributed to Donald Trump.
374. Jill Colvin, "Donald Trump a 'Blue-Collar Billionaire' with a Lot of Money," *Associated Press*, July 18, 2016, https://apnews.com/24939b966d8942cd8f82e1b6234368ef.
375. Susan Jones, "155,215,000: Record Number of Americans Employed," *CNSNews*, March 9, 2018, https://www.cnsnews.com/news/article/susan-jones/155215000-number-employed-americans-sets-8th-record-trump-era.
376. Paul R. La Monica, "Black Unemployment Rate Hits a Record Low," *CNN Business*, June 1, 2018, https://money.cnn.com/2018/06/01/news/economy/black-unemployment-rate-record-low/index.html.
377. "Food Stamp Use down Big League under Trump—Over 3 Million Off the Dole," *Political Insider*, August 3, 2018, https://thepoliticalinsider.com/trump-food-stamps-3-million/.
378. Dominic Rushe, "US Economy Growing at Annual Rate of 4.1%, Fastest Pace in Four Years," *Guardian*, July 27, 2018, https://www.theguardian.com/business/2018/jul/27/us-economy-report-second-quarter-commerce-department.

379. Julie Allen, "NATO Members Increase Defence Spending by $100 Billion after Donald Trump Called Them 'Delinquents'," *Telegraph*, January 27, 2019, https://www.telegraph.co.uk/news/2019/01/27/nato-members-increase-defence-spending-100-billion-donald-trump/.
380. Jamie McIntyre, "Here's How Much Ground ISIS Has Lost since Trump Took Over," *Washington Examine*, December 23, 2017, https://www.washingtonexaminer.com/heres-how-much-ground-isis-has-lost-since-trump-took-over.
381. Dave Boyer, "Trump Signs Defense Policy Bill That Rebuilds Military, Boosts Troop Pay," *Washington Times*, August 13, 2018, https://www.washingtontimes.com/news/2018/aug/13/donald-trump-signs-new-defense-policy-bill-rebuild/.
382. Ariane Mandell, "Netanyahu Thanks Trump for Keeping Promises, Moving Embassy to Jerusalem," *Jerusalem Post*, May 14, 2018, https://www.jpost.com/Israel-News/WATCH-LIVE-America-completes-historic-embassy-move-to-Jerusalem-556364.
383. Erin McCarthy Holliday, "President Trump Signs Criminal Justice Reform First Step Act into Law," *Jurist*, December 21, 2018, https://www.jurist.org/news/2018/12/president-trump-signs-criminal-justice-reform-first-step-act-into-law/.
384. Thomas Carroll, "Trump's School Choice Victory Is Just the Beginning," *The Hill*, December 31, 2017, https://thehill.com/opinion/healthcare/366886-trumps-school-choice-victory-is-just-the-beginning.
385. "Trump Just Achieved What Every President since Nixon Had Promised: Energy Independence," *Investor's Business Daily*, December 7, 2018, https://www.investors.com/politics/editorials/energy-independence-trump/.
386. Sergio Chapa, "Oil Prices End Year with First Annual Decline since 2015," *Houston Chronicle*, December 31, 2018, https://www.houstonchronicle.com/business/energy/article/Oil-prices-end-year-with-first-annual-decline-13500595.php. When the price of oil and gas decline, and when coal us used to generate electricity, the cost of electricity to the consumer declines.
387. Samuel Smith, "White House Hosts 100 Evangelical Leaders for State-Like Dinner: 'This Is Spiritual Warfare,'" *Christian Post*, August 28, 2018, https://www.christianpost.com/news/white-house-hosts-100-evangelical-leaders-state-like-dinner-this-is-spiritual-warfare.html.
388. Josh Delk, "Pence: 'There's Prayer on a Regular Basis in This White House,'" *The Hill*, May 3, 2018, https://thehill.com/homenews/administration/386158-pence-theres-prayer-on-a-regular-basis-in-this-white-house.
389. "New Executive Order Aims to Protect Religious Liberty from Government Overreach," Religious News Service, May 2, 2018, https://religionnews.com/2018/05/02/trump-to-sign-executive-order-creating-new-white-house-faith-based-initiative/.

390. Alex Williams, "Franklin Graham: Donald Trump Has Defended Christianity More than Any President in My Lifetime," Premier Christian Radio, January 23, 2018, https://www.premierchristianradio.com/News/World/Franklin-Graham-Donald-Trump-has-defended-Christianity-more-than-any-president-in-my-lifetime.
391. Erica L. Green, Katie Benner and Robert Pear, "'Transgender' Could Be Defined Out of Existence under Trump Administration," *New York Times*, October 21, 2018, https://www.nytimes.com/2018/10/21/us/politics/transgender-trump-administration-sex-definition.html.
392. Julia Manchester, "Maxine Waters Calls on People to Confront Trump Officials in Public Spaces," *The Hill*, June 24, 2018, https://thehill.com/homenews/house/393874-maxine-waters-calls-on-supporters-to-confront-trump-officials-in-public-spaces.

CHAPTER 14, GOING ON OFFENSE

393. Rodney Hawkins, "Biden Tells African-American Audience GOP Ticket Would Put Them "Back in Chains," *CBS News*, August 14, 2012, https://www.cbsnews.com/news/biden-tells-african-american-audience-gop-ticket-would-put-them-back-in-chains/.
394. This radio ad was broadcast repeatedly over black radio stations in Missouri by the Missouri Democratic Party in November 1998 with an intent of spiking the black vote by terrorizing black voters. The ad was rebroadcast on the Sean Hannity Show on the Fox News Channel on August 12, 2019.
395. John 8:32, (God's Word translation, Holy Bible).
396. "Pennsylvania Statewide," Axiom Strategies, www.RemingtonResearchGroup.com. Survey conducted November 1 through November 2, 2016. 2,683 likely General Election voters participated in the survey. Survey weighted to match expected turnout demographics for the 2016 General Election. Margin of Error is ±1.89% with a 95% level of confidence. Totals do not always equal 100% due to rounding.
397. "2016 Democratic Party Platform, as Approved by the Democratic Platform Committee July 8-9, 2016, Orlando, Florida," https://democrats.org/wp-content/uploads/2018/10/2016_DNC_Platform.pdf.
398. Jonathan Martin and Alan Blinder, "Second Virginia Democrat Says He Wore Blackface, Throwing Party into Turmoil," *New York Times*, February 6, 2019, https://www.nytimes.com/2019/02/06/us/politics/virginia-blackface-mark-herring.html.
399. Debra Heine, "Turning Point USA's Candace Owens Smacks down Black Lives Matter," PJ Media, April 22, 2018, https://pjmedia.com/trending/tpusas-candace-owens-smacks-black-lives-matter-kanye-likes-sees/.
400. Jennifer Harper, "How Americans Really Feel about the Mainstream Media," *Washington Times*, September 12, 2018, https://www washingtontimes.com/news/2018/sep/12/how-americans-really-feel-about-mainstream-media/.

401. Jillian Kay Melchior, "Meet the Woman Rashida Tlaib Called a 'Prop,'" *Wall Street Journal*, March 29, 2019, https://www.wsj.com/articles/meet-the-woman-rashida-tlaib-called-a-prop-11553899222.
402. Kyle Olson, "1986: Trump, Rosa Parks, Muhammad Ali Received 'Ellis Island' Award," American Mirror, September 4, 2016, http://www.theamericanmirror.com/1986-trump-received-ellis-island-award-along-rosa-parks-muhammad-ali/.
403. Anderson Cooper, "Alexandria Ocasio-Cortez: The Rookie Congresswoman Challenging the Democratic Establishment," *CBS 60 Minutes*, January 6, 2019, https://www.cbsnews.com/news/alexandria-ocasio-cortez-the-rookie-congresswoman-challenging-the-democratic-establishment-60-minutes-interview-full-transcript-2019-01-06/.
404. Dinesh D'Souza, "Richard Spencer, Wilsonian Progressive," American Greatness, August 10, 2018, https://amgreatness.com/2018/08/10/richard-spencer-wilsonian-progressive/.
405. Danielle Kurtzleben, "Trump Touts Low Unemployment Rates for African-Americans, Hispanics," *NPR Fact Check*, January 8, 2018, https://www.npr.org/2018/01/08/576552028/fact-check-trump-touts-low-unemployment-rates-for-african-americans-hispanics.
406. Bowen Xiao, "Trump Signs Criminal Justice Reform Bill into Law," *Epoch Times*, December 21, 2018, https://www.theepochtimes.com/trump-signs-criminal-justice-reform-bill-into-law_2745833.html.
407. Kolbe Nelson, "Alexandria Ocasio-Cortez Says 'No Question' Trump Is a Racist in 60 Minutes Interview," *60 Minutes Overtime*, January 6, 2019, https://www.cbsnews.com/news/alexandria-ocasio-cortez-calls-president-trump-a-racist-in-60-minutes-interview-2019-01-06/.

CHAPTER 15, COMING HOME

408. Shandira Pavelcik, "The African American Middle Class," Black Demographics, February 17, 2013, https://blackdemographics.com/households/middle-class/.
409. Kayla Fontenot, Jessica Semega, and Melissa Kollar, "Income and Poverty in the United States: 2017," U.S. Census Bureau publication, September 2018, 12, table 3.
410. George S. Schuyler, *Black and Conservative* (New Rochelle: Arlington House, 1966).
411. "Flashback—Clarence Thomas: 'It's a High-Tech Lynching for Uppity Blacks'," *CNS News*, September 17, 2018, https://www.cnsnews.com/news/article/cnsnewscom-staff/flashback-clarence-thomas-denies-anita-hill-allegations-calls-senate.
412. "Black Support for Nominee Rises," *Chicago Tribune*, October 15, 1991, https://www.chicagotribune.com/news/ct-xpm-1991-10-15-9104030243-story.html.
413. "Voting and Registration in the Election of November 2016," United States Census Bureau, May 2017, table 2, https://www.census.gov/data/tables/time-series/demo/voting-and-registration/p20-580.html. Number

arrived at by multiplying the number of registered black Americans who voted by 8%, the percent of the black vote commonly attributed to Donald Trump.

414. Nancy J. Weiss, *Farewell to the Party of Lincoln* (Princeton: Princeton University Press, 1983), 193.
415. *Ibid.*
416. Sarah Le, "Blexit Rally Emboldens Conservative Minorities in Los Angeles," *Epoch Times*, January 20, 2019, https://www.theepochtimes.com/blexit-rally-emboldens-conservative-minorities-in-los-angeles_2773708.html.
417. *Ibid.*
418. *Ibid.*
419. *Ibid.*
420. Phillip Bump, "The Fix: When Did Black Americans Start Voting So Heavily Democratic," *Washington Post*, July 7, 2015, https://www.washingtonpost.com/news/the-fix/wp/2015/07/07/when-did-black-americans-start-voting-so-heavily-democratic/?noredirect=on&utm_term=.36e7971fc56f.

CHAPTER 16, ORGANIZING FOR VICTORY

421. Textbook was likely used as a supplemental text. In this book, Smith contends that ideological conservatism and racism "are and always have been equivalent in the United States." Robert C. Smith, *Conservatism and Racism, and Why in America They Are the Same* (Albany: State University of New York Press, 2010).
422. "Textbook Says Trump Is Mentally Ill, Supporters are Racists," *Fox News Channel*, April 17, 2018, video, https://video.foxnews.com/v/5771798160001/#sp=show-clips; the textbook is *By the People: A History of the United States*, published by Pearson Education.
423. David W. Southern, *The Progressive Era and Race: Reaction and Reform, 1900-1917* (Wheeling: Harlan Davidson, Inc., 2005), 24.
424. "Democrat Legislator Demands Black Babies Be Exempt from Heartbeat Laws," Pulpit & Pen, April 20, 2019, https://pulpitandpen.org/2019/04/20/democrat-legislator-demands-black-babies-be-exempt-from-heartbeat-laws/.
425. Richard Nadler, "Republican Issue Advertising in Black and Hispanic Population Areas: A Meta-Study of the 2002 Mid-Term Election," *Access Communications Group*, February 2003, 26.
426. Greg Price, "Fox News's Audience Almost Exclusively White as Network Faces Backlash over Immigration Coverage," *Newsweek*, August 10, 2018, https://www.newsweek.com/fox-news-white-audience-immigration-1067807.
427. Elizabeth Thomas and Abby Cruz, "More 2020 Democrats Calling Trump a 'White Supremacist,'" *ABC News*, August 9, 2019, https://abcnews.go.com/Politics/2020-democrats-calling-trump-white-supremacist/story?id=64885082.

428. Benjamin Carson and Candy Carson, *America the Beautiful* (Grand Rapids: Zondervan, 2012), 156.
429. *Ibid.*, 156.
430. Jason Riley, "Why Trump Shouldn't Write Off Black Vote," *Wall Street Journal*, August 2, 2016.
431. Noah Friedman, Josh Barro, and Lamar Salter, "'The Apprentice' Helped Trump Win Approval of African-Americans and Latinos—Here's How He Lost It," *Business Insider*, July 18, 2017, https://www.businessinsider.com/trump-popular-black-hispanic-apprentice-birther-joshua-green-devils-bargain-2017-7.
432. Jason Riley, "Why Trump Shouldn't Write Off Black Vote," *Wall Street Journal*, August 2, 2016.
433. Jim Tankersley, "Trump to Steer More Money to 'Opportunity Zones'," *New York Times*, December 12, 2018, https://www.nytimes.com/2018/12/12/us/politics/trump-opportunity-zones-tax-cut.html.
434. Editorial Board, "We Assume It Was Pure Motives That Led a Trump Supporter to Launch a Cleanup in Cummings' District, Right?," *Baltimore Sun*, August 6, 2019, https://www.baltimoresun.com/opinion/editorial/bs-ed-0808-conservatives-clean-west-baltimore-20190806-hmc2gndnhfhodch4yxromipgnq-story.html.
435. Jim Hoft, "'Thank You, Mr. Trump!'—Baltimore Residents Thank President after Conservatives Come in to Help Clean Up Community," Gateway Pundit, August 5, 2019, https://www.thegatewaypundit.com/2019/08/thank-you-mr-trump-baltimore-residents-thank-president-after-conservatives-come-in-to-help-clean-up-community/.
436. Nancy J. Weiss, *Farewell to the Party of Lincoln* (Princeton: Princeton University Press, 1983), 193.
437. *Ibid.*, 201.
438. Richard Nadler, "Republican Issue Advertising in Black and Hispanic Population Areas, a Meta-Study of the 2002 Election," *Access Communications Group*, February 2003, 24.
439. *Ibid.*, 5.
440. Rasmussen poll read by Vernon Robinson, a North Carolina resident.
441. As National Director of the National Draft Ben Carson for President Committee Vernon Robinson was in charge of running these ads. Performance data and results were recorded by Robinson.
442. *Ibid.*
443. *Ibid.*
444. The 2016 Committee was the super PAC successor to the National Draft Ben Carson for President Committee. In 2017 The 2016 Committee morphed into the Stars and Stripes Forever super PAC.
445. "Population Estimates, July 1, 2018, (V2018)," United States Census Bureau, https://www.census.gov/quickfacts/pa; "Voting and Registration in the Election of November 2016," United States Census Bureau, https://www.census.gov/data/tables/time-series/demo/voting-and-registration/p20-580.html. Population of Pennsylvania 12,807,060, 11.9% black

Americans, 74.5% of black population registered to vote, 59.4% black voting participation in 2016 election, 21% vote for Trump by black Pennsylvania voters = 141,631 black votes for Donald Trump. "Pennsylvania Statewide," Axiom Strategies, www.RemingtonResearch Group.com. Survey conducted November 1 through November 2, 2016, 21% of black voters indicated they intended to vote for Donald Trump.

446. As National Director of the National Draft Ben Carson for President Committee Vernon Robinson was in charge of running these ads. Performance data and results were recorded by Robinson.
447. Information provided to Vernon Robinson by the committees involved.
448. *Ibid.*
449. *Ibid.*
450. Center for Medical Progress, http://www.centerformedicalprogress.org/cmp/investigative-footage/.
451. Information provided by Tom Donelson, America's PAC, to Vernon Robinson. Donelson was an associate of the late Richard Nadler at Access Communications.

APPENDIX

452. *Ibid.*
453. Scott Jennings, "Ralph Northam Should Be Remembered for Advocating the Slaughtering of Deformed Babies," *USA Today*, February 5, 2019, https://www.usatoday.com/story/opinion/2019/02/05/ralph-northam-advocating-abortion-infanticide-worse-than-blackface-column/2776498002/.
454. Harry Enten, "Trump Has Gained among Black Voters since the 2016 Election," *CNN*, August 18, 2018, https://www.cnn.com/2018/08/18/politics/poll-of-the-week-trump-black-voters/index.html.
455. Anne Gearan and Abby Phillip, "Clinton Regrets 1996 Remark on 'Super Predators' after Encounter with Activist," *Washington Post*, February 25, 2016, https://www.washingtonpost.com/news/post-politics/wp/2016/02/25/clinton-heckled-by-black-lives-matter-activist/?utm_term=.7fffa05db65a.
456. Christina Caron and Liam Stack, "Maryland House of Delegates Censures Mary Ann Lisanti for Using Racist Slur," *New York Times*, February 28, 2019, https://www.nytimes.com/2019/02/28/us/politics/mary-ann-lisanti-racism.html.
457. Mark Whitehouse, "Here's One Way Racial Inequality Is Declining," *Bloomberg Opinion*, August 3, 2018, https://www.bloomberg.com/opinion/articles/2018-08-03/u-s-employment-gap-between-blacks-and-whites-hits-record-low.
458. Quin Hillyer, "Pennsylvania and Texas Show Vote Fraud Is Real," *Washington Examiner*, January 31, 2019, https://www.washingtonexaminer.com/opinion/noncitizens-registered-to-vote-in-pennsylvania-and-texas-show-vote-fraud-is-real; "*The Heritage Foundation recently undertook an effort to find and record as many instances of voter fraud as*

possible in all 50 States. In a report they released documenting recorded instances of voter fraud across the country, more than 1,177 proven cases of voter fraud were confirmed . . . ". Bethany Day, "Time to Take Voter Fraud Seriously," *AMAC Magazine* 13, no. 21.

459. John Binder, "Watch—Antifa Chants Death to America: 'No Borders! No Wall! No USA at All!'," *Breitbart*, August 12, 2018, https://www.breitbart.com/politics/2018/08/12/watch-antifa-chants-death-to-america-no-borders-no-wall-no-usa-at-all/.

Index

About the Authors

VERNON ROBINSON III has lived the American Dream; growing up on the Southside of Los Angeles, excelling in academics while playing varsity basketball at University High School made possible by a voluntary bussing program, earning the rank of Eagle Scout in the late great Boy Scouts of America, graduating from the United States Air Force Academy, serving on active duty, teaching at a historically black university, serving in public office, leading the school choice movement in North Carolina, and finally drafting Ben Carson for President. Robinson was co-founder of Black Americans to Re-Elect the President, a hybrid political action committee, where he now serves as Treasurer.

Commissioned a Second Lieutenant in the Air Force, Robinson served as Missile Combat Crew Commander in Strategic Air Command. He was assigned to the 15th Air Force where his Tuskegee Airman father served 35 years before. During active duty, Robinson was responsible for the execution of emergency nuclear war orders from the national command authority. Robinson is active in veterans' affairs promoting veterans' coffees to facilitate comradeship and the dissemination of critical information to veterans of all branches and service periods.

Robinson became politically active because of the deplorable condition of educational opportunity in North Carolina particularly for children from lower income families. His public life has been dedicated to helping others take advantage of the opportunity that is America. Working with former North Carolina Speaker Tempore Steven Ray Wood, Robinson championed and ultimately saw the ratification of legislation that authorized charter schools. Robinson administered a privately funded lower income scholarship program to demonstrate the demand for publicly funded scholarships in grades K-12. Two decades later the Republican majority passed publicly funded scholarships for 18,000 lower income students. When he ran for State Superintendent of Public Instruction in 1996, Robinson won the GOP nomination, the only black candidate to ever defeat a white opponent in a North Carolina GOP primary statewide since Reconstruction.

Robinson served eight years on the Winston-Salem City Council as Alderman of the South Ward and Vice Chairman of the Public Safety Committee. An early conservative supporter of criminal justice reform, Robinson supported changes in police procedure to ensure exculpatory evidence was shared with both prosecution and defendants.

Robinson's consulting firm, Robinson Stratavision Consulting LLC, helps clients build large interactive organizations. His greatest professional achievement was directing the campaign to draft Ben Carson for President. During his two year effort, $18 million was raised, and 39,000 volunteers executed 900 events in only the second successful conservative grassroots presidential draft in American history.

Robinson is married, has three children and one grandchild. He is an avid wargamer and student of military history.

BRUCE EBERLE has a passion for freedom and for America. His dream is to see an America that is not divided into groups, but unified as one people enjoying the American dream. His life has been spent raising funds for conservative candidates and organizations. Along with his wife Kathi, he founded the Eberle Communications Group in 1974. ECG has raised more than a billion dollars for conservative causes and other worthwhile organizations. He served as Ronald Reagan's fund raiser in his first run for president in 1976.

Bruce has spoken a number of times at the International School of Fund Raising in England and Spain. He is the author of the widely regarded book, *Political Direct Mail Fund Raising* that has gone through six printings.

Bruce has been a conservative activist throughout his life. He served as local chapter chairman, state chairman, and national director of Young Americans for Freedom. In 1980, Bruce served as co-chairman of the Draft Jack Kemp for Vice President Committee. In 2016, it was Bruce's idea to draft Dr. Ben Carson to run for president, and he got fully behind that effort, not only raising funds, but also assisting John Phillip Sousa with the writing of *Rx for America*. More than 1.3 million copies of that book were printed, sold, and distributed. For a number of years, Bruce wrote a weekly blog advocating free markets, individual responsibility, and individual freedom.

He is a recipient of the Nehemiah award for leadership from Youth for Tomorrow (YFT), a residence home for at-risk boys and girls, and the Pro Gloria Dei award from Wisconsin Lutheran College (WLC). Bruce is a trustee of YFT, a Regent at WLC, and was a founder of Time of Grace Ministry, an international Christian evangelism organization. Bruce and his wife, Kathi, co-chair an annual gala to benefit Grace Christian Academy, a special school that provides a high quality education for the children of poor families who would not otherwise be able to do so.

Bruce is a graduate in engineering, and a military veteran. He and his wife Kathi have two children, and four wonderful grandsons.